BELONGING MATTERS

Conversations on Adoption, Family, and Kinship

Julie Ryan McGue

Printed in the United States of America

Hardcover ISBN: 978-1-958714-80-5
Paperback ISBN: 978-1-958714-81-2
Ebook ISBN: 978-1-958714-82-9
Library of Congress Control Number: 2023931354

Muse Literary
3319 N. Cicero Avenue
Chicago IL 60641-9998

To Steve
You made my life better.

TABLE OF CONTENTS

"I am out with lanterns looking for myself."
—Emily Dickinson

*   *   *

"A sense of belonging is not physical.
We can't find it by changing where we live or what we do.
We have to carry it within us."
—P. C. Cast

FOREWORD

Every writer creates a work of art, a story, or a book: Not everyone creates a conversation. With *Twice a Daughter* and now *Belonging Matters*, Julie McGue has established a dialogue with strangers all over the world who regard her as a friend, an ally, a fellow human being.

The poet David Whyte implores us to "give up all the other worlds except the one you belong in." As Julie McGue points out, the issue for adoptees in closed adoptions is knowing which world that is. That's why *Belonging Matters* is essential reading. She traces the arc of adoptees as we become adept at adaptation; how we intuitively manage the transition from biological to adoptive parents. In the process, though inadvertently, we become experts on living in exile — to ourselves and to some extent, as the essayist notes, to society at large.

The author's curiosity, open-mindedness and relentless drive toward her truth is the salve that resolves this state of suspension, of occupying a foreign land. Come along as Julie takes us on her quest to higher ground with keen observation and insight. Whether it's about her pajama clad slumber party, being a twin adoptee, or reacting to her own child's decimation of the tulip garden, every vignette begets a sense of rekindling. What is the element in the event, scene or memory that truly matters? Julie probes until she finds the light within.

It is the hero's journey to discover the world in which we belong. That's true for all of us, but more acutely for one who has additional obstacles and obfuscations put in her path. Julie writes about removing these obstacles, dismantling artifice, and unearthing core messages. From her emotional center, her determined spirit and her finely tuned intellect, we glean her attunement, and the reader becomes in turn more discerning of invisible essences.

Belonging in the world correlates with the inner symmetry Julie explores. Derived precisely because of its lack, through a life that could be described as comfortable yet without a compass, she's had no idea that she is lost. The remotest signal from the inner self is Julie's lifelong urge to write, record, and capture herself in her journal. Now as she flowers as an author, speaker, blogger, and advocate, Julie extends that internal conversation to us.

Each of *Belonging Matters'* chapters offers a parable. That generosity reveals the extent of Julie's outward-facing desire for connection. Through relatable language, Julie recounts poignant episodes with her ineffable twin sister, shares lessons learned, and draws us toward universal revelations. The remarkable irony is that someone so deprived of access to an indigenous family as she was, has connected to such a global matrix of belonging. In doing so, Julie has created a world for herself and an inclusive place for others to reside.

No matter where we are on this ineradicable path, *Belonging Matters* lends a helping hand.

Diane Dewey
Author of *Fixing the Fates*

AUTHOR'S NOTE

For most of my life, my adoption was tucked neatly behind a fascinating fact: I have a twin sister.

My sister and I have looked so much alike that relatives, neighbors, and classmates were often confused about which name went with which sister. When my adoptive parents picked up my three-week-old twin sister and me from St. Vincent's Orphanage in Chicago, they were told we were fraternal twins. In 2011, DNA proved we are not fraternal twins. We are identical.

The people we encountered did not just marvel at our similar appearance, gestures, speech, and habits; they were mesmerized. Often we were ordered to stand next to one another so the onlooker could judge who was taller, heavier, or had more freckles. As irritating and embarrassing as it was to have this happen regularly, it was also a relief. I was grateful for my twindom. It served as the perfect smokescreen for something I was uncomfortable thinking about and discussing: my adoption.

My sister and I knew at an early age that we were adopted as infants. In 1959, my adoptive parents didn't dwell on Adoption Day, the day we joined our new family. Instead, my family celebrated our birthday, the day we were born. And every so often, after the cake and presents had been stowed away, our folks would call my sister and me into the living room. They would express how much they cared about us, how dearly they had wanted us, and that they would support us if we ever wanted to look into our adoption.

Beyond those "check-ins," our adoption was rarely brought up. Occasionally, when my folks entertained at home, one of their friends would remark, "You girls have gotten so tall. Why, I remember when your folks brought you home from St. Vincent's." These "adoption conversations" brought a heated flush to my cheeks. I didn't like being different or having it recognized in such a public way. I wanted to fit in, to belong. When my parents' friends reminded me that I came from another set of parents, my face and neck flushed a flamingo pink.

When I was old enough to have sleepovers, I snuggled into my sleeping bag in a darkened rec room and whispered secrets with my school friends. On one occasion, one of the girls summoned the courage to ask, "You guys are adopted, right?" Within seconds, my flannel PJs were drenched in sweat. Embarrassment steamed up my sleeping bag.

I abhorred this question, "You're adopted, right?" It was an unbidden intrusion into my privacy. Mostly, I hated this query because it meant my friends, and likely their parents too, had been gossiping about my family and me behind our backs.

To my friend on that sleepover night, I offered a quiet "Yeah." I suspected another equally dreaded question would soon follow.

"So, what happened to your *real* parents?" my friend quizzed.

After this incident I was prepared. Whenever the "adoption conversation" came up with my friends, I rattled off a well-rehearsed response. "Yeah, I'm adopted. I've always known about it. And I don't know anything about where I came from.

Mom and Dad are my *real* parents." I spewed all this out and changed the subject.

As I look back on those uncomfortable episodes, I believe they have stuck with me because of unrecognized shame. Even though it wasn't my fault, I was embarrassed I knew nothing about my background, my birth parents, or why I had been placed for adoption. It was a shortcoming—one that I had no control over and one that I couldn't rectify because of stringent state closed adoption laws. When I compared myself with friends and family members, I always came up lacking in the personal history department.

What's more? After someone posed any variation of those uncomfortable adoption questions, I had the sense that they viewed me differently than before. When I wasn't looking, I felt them studying me. I imagined what they were thinking: "What is it about you that's different? Is it that you are adopted or that you are a twin?"

Until I wrote *Twice a Daughter*, my memoir about searching for birth relatives, I wondered, "What is it about me? Is it my adoption that sets me apart, or is it my twindom? And where do I belong?" Unlike that shy, weary preteen in her sleeping bag, I have spent a lot of time reflecting upon "What is it about me?" It is only now that I am a middle-aged woman in reunion with birth relatives that I'm open to discussing my adoption experience, my sense of family, and where I belong.

I have come to view my adoption and being a twin as inseparable. The intersection of these two vital details has formed my identity and defines my existence. As a mature adult, I embrace both of these truths. Frankly, it's a relief to no longer allow my adoption to take a second seat to my twindom.

My closed adoption experience, the unique bonds I hold with my twin sister and kin—my adoptive and birth families—and the relationships I maintain with my immediate family, friends, and community are at the heart of this collection of essays. I believe the answers to the fundamental questions *what is it about you* and *where do you belong* lie in our nature, formative experiences, relationships, and connection to the communities in which we thrive.

This collection is about the pursuit of identity, embracing all of who we have come to be, finding meaning in difficult experiences, and discerning with whom and where we belong. Belonging is fundamental to our personal development. It is what nourishes our spirit, fuels us with purpose, and compels us to soar beyond limitations. Belonging matters.

Section I

ADOPTION

ARE YOU MY MOTHER?

Are You My Mother? is a 1960s children's book by P. D. Eastman. It's about a baby bird. The tale begins with the mother leaving the nest and flying off to find food. When the baby bird hatches, he doesn't understand where his mother has gone. Too young to fly, he sets off on foot. He asks a kitten, a hen, a dog, and a cow if they are his mother. He's disappointed when none of them are. Eventually, his mother returns and the two are reunited.

For most young children, Are You My Mother? is a cute story with an entertaining plot, a myriad of animals, and clever line drawings. If the audience is an adopted child, the story contains a deeper meaning. For an adoptee, especially one who is a product of closed adoption, Are You My Mother? might have a subtitle: where is my mother, why did she leave me, and why can't I know my "personal history"?

This is the dilemma of the child placed for adoption in the second half of the last century under the closed adoption system. For adoptees like me who develop health concerns as adults, this dilemma can have medical consequences as they spend years asking people to help them find their mothers.

WHAT IS CLOSED ADOPTION?

My twin sister and I were adopted during the Baby Scoop Era—post–World War II through the early 1970s—when birth moms were not involved in the adoption process. Adoption agencies were charged with matching babies with adoptive parents. Other than the presumption that their child would go to a family with the same religious preference, birth parents were not privy to the prospective parent list. They weren't offered a say-so, and they didn't expect to weigh in. Once the relinquishment papers were signed, birth parents were prohibited from all future contact with their birth child.

When it was clear that my twenty-six-year-old birth mother was pregnant, and my birth dad wasn't going to marry her, she and a close friend left their hometown for Chicago. There, my mother met with a Catholic Charities social worker for an intake interview.

In 2010, I petitioned the agency for the non-identifying information in my adoption file. I learned my birth parents were both teachers at the same elementary school and were involved in a relationship; they argued extensively about religion and forced marriage; a Protestant, my birth dad refused to convert to Catholicism. In those days, it was unacceptable for a Catholic to marry a non-Catholic. In the interview, my mother also disclosed that her parents would disown her if they learned of her predicament. Without a spouse or familial support, my birth mom was forced into adoption. Because of her Catholic faith, abortion was out of the question.

In the 1950s, society judged unwed mothers harshly. Unmarried women who found themselves "in the family way" were considered serious sinners, people of low values and morals. Parents of unwed mothers shunned, hid, or sent their daughters away until the pregnancy was over. Often, these women were not welcomed back home. Some became permanently estranged from their families.

In that 1958 intake interview with the Catholic Charities social worker, my mother admitted she felt deep shame, regret, and humiliation. Her overriding fear was she would be found out. The social worker encouraged my mother to take an alias, and she welcomed the idea. The false identity protected her against anyone—especially her parents and large family—from learning about her situation. For adoption purposes, assuming an alias was entirely legal. The fake name my mother chose appears on my original birth record (OBR), a detail that made it difficult for me to locate her when I needed to do so.

During her pregnancy, my birth mother lived in a women's home in Chicago. During her stay there, she did not meet other women who had already made the adoption journey; she received only basic prenatal care; and she did not create an adoption hospital plan, as birth mothers in open adoption now do.

The social worker at the adoption agency had given my mother more advice: once your child is born, it's best if you do not see or hold your baby to avoid forming an attachment. On a frigid February day in 1959, my birth mom went to the women's hospital on the south side of Chicago and labored alone. A few days later, she signed the surrender of parental rights without ever seeing or holding my sister and me, and then she returned to her teaching job as if nothing had happened.

Much like my birth mother, birth moms in the Baby Scoop Era did not realize that after they relinquished their child, they would experience intense feelings of loss and grief. Most were not given the necessary tools or resources to cope with these acute emotions. Instead of receiving counseling or sharing their experience with friends or family, they suffered in silence. Ann Fessler details the dilemma of the closed adoption birth mother in her 2006 book *The Girls Who Went Away: The Hidden History of Women Who Surrendered Children for Adoption in the Decades Before Roe v. Wade.*

It was quite common during this period of adoption history for adoption agencies to collect only rudimentary information from the birth mom. Height, weight, hair and eye color, education, and religious preference were usually noted. When I received the information from my adoption file, I learned that, at the time of her pregnancy, my mother was in good health and my father wore glasses. That was it. No mention was made of medical histories to be aware of or health conditions to guard against. Nor was there an addendum put into the file when family health issues popped up later in my birth parents' lives. When the family court judge finalized my adoption eight months later, it was as if my slate was wiped clean and my biological background was deemed irrelevant.

Another curious practice during this era was that birth mothers were not required to reveal the birth father's identity. During this time, the disregard for a birth father's parental rights was legal. Bypassing this step meant a closed adoption could move faster through the court system. On my original birth record in the space where my birth dad's name should appear are the words *legally omitted*. This was another common practice in a closed adoption. My fellow adoptees and I joke that we all have the same birth father: Mr. Legally Omitted.

Because I lacked my birth father's name, I had to locate my birth mother first. The timing of my search was perfect. In 2011, Illinois' adoption statutes underwent an overhaul. An adoptee born after 1947 was now allowed to request their OBR, and a state-appointed confidential intermediary program was instituted. The intermediary could petition the courts for adoption documents that had been sealed for decades. I got lucky again. Not only was my birth mother's alias in my file, so was her true identity. Over time, both of my birth parents complied with my request for information.

Now that I'm in reunion with birth relatives, I believe if the "open" adoption process—which came into vogue in the early 1980s—had been available to my birth mom, our lives would have been filled with less trauma and more joy. I might have been spared the angst of searching for years for a woman who feared being found. In turn, my mother might have shared my family background with me long before my health demanded it as a middle-aged woman.

ARE THERE BENEFITS TO CLOSED ADOPTION?

Perhaps like me, you wonder if there are benefits to closed adoption. Even though I'd been placed into a nurturing family and raised with my twin sister, I never stopped wondering why I'd been adopted and where my *other family* had gone.

To recap, closed adoption refers to an adoption process in which there is no interaction between birth families and prospective adoptive parents, or between the birth parents and the adopted child/adult. As a result, no identifying information is shared between any members of the adoption triad: birth parent, adoptive parent, and adoptee. Rudimentary non-identifying information such as physical attributes, amount of education, and basic health details is often available, but it's up to the discretion of the agency facilitating the adoption to disseminate it. State adoption statutes control when and if these restrictions change.

In contrast, birth parents in open adoption are given extensive counseling about what to expect before, during, and after adoption is finalized. They select their baby's adoptive parents and develop their child's adoption plan with the prospective parents. Unlike the closed adoption birth mother, in an open adoption the mother can remain a part of her child's life if she chooses.

The adoptee in an open adoption has many more benefits than in closed adoption, too. The child is given the birth family's background and medical history, understands why they were placed for adoption, and can maintain contact with their first family if all parties agree. Counseling about identity, family, and belonging is often provided by the adoption agency.

The advantages of the closed adoption experience vary for members of the adoption constellation. Many birth parents claim that they benefit from closed adoption because it provides closure; they feel they can move on with their lives. For birth mothers who wish to avoid explaining their decision to others, closed adoption provides privacy and eases feelings of fear and vulnerability. And the lack of contact between birth and adoptive families eliminates co-parenting issues. Closed adoption provides the adoptive child protection from unstable birth families and eliminates potential co-parenting issues.

Given my conversations with my birth mom, as well as the sessions with birth mothers in my post-adoption support group, the above points about closure and privacy and family-building make sense. Yet, I find the above list lacking. It doesn't address the adoptee's need for identity.

To achieve a full sense of self, adoption must provide the adoptee access to family background, medical history, and genealogy. From where I sit, closed adoption benefitted the birth and adoptive parents and left the adoptee behind. The responsibility to change this lopsided paradigm lands squarely on adoption agencies and state legislatures. The "right to know" should not take a second seat to the "right to privacy," especially since the full and healthy psychological development of an individual is at risk.

WHAT IS POSITIVE ADOPTION LANGUAGE (PAL)?

A friend of mine, who has a son she adopted thirty years ago, recently corrected me. In one of my weekly blog posts I referred to my situation—an adoptee from the closed adoption era—as having been "given up for adoption." In my defense, this was a commonly used term in the 1950s and '60s, but the nomenclature surrounding adoption has changed a lot since then. My friend pointed out that the correct language is now "placed for adoption."

While I didn't argue with my friend, I don't agree.

As an adoptee, I consider myself as having been "given up" because something was given up during my adoption. I lost all sense of who I'd been and from where I came because of the rigors of closed adoption. And until 2011, Illinois adoption statutes blocked my "right to know." I was a mature adult when I learned my personal history—that's a lot of living without knowing the basic circumstances of one's existence.

From an adoptive parent's point of view, I understand how "placed for adoption" sounds more positive than "given up." But the well-meaning comment from my friend left me wondering if this more modern, positive adoptive language just sanitizes a complex situation. Like any topic, it depends on which side of the controversy you sit.

The change in adoption language came as a result of adoption reform in the 1970s.

Even as an adoptee, I find it easy to get tripped up about the correct terms to use. Some adoption terms to avoid include: unwanted pregnancy, real parent/mother/father, natural parent/mother/father/child, illegitimate child, give up/put up for adoption, give away, adopted out, abandoned, surrendered, and adoption triangle.

The advised positive adoption language utilitizes these labels instead: unintended pregnancy, birth or biological parent/mother/father/child, child placed for adoption, born to unmarried parents, make an adoption plan, choose adoption, terminated parental rights, was adopted, and adoption triad.

In a nutshell, adoptive parents seek to banish the negative attitudes and connotations inherent in adoption's definition and history, while adoptees don't want the negative aspects of their adoption glossed over.

So how do we resolve this controversy?

What's important is the continued dialogue. I would have welcomed improved communication with my adoptive parents about any or all aspects of my adoption: identity, belonging, rejection, loss, and search and reunion. My adoptive parents came from the era of "if we don't talk about it, it didn't happen," but that mindset creates confusion, promotes lack of understanding, and hinders relationship building. The more we talk about the need for acceptable adoption language, the better we understand our perspective and those held by others.

WHO IS THE "IDEAL ADOPTEE"?

Adoptees, in terms of how we view our adoption, come in as many different flavors as are found in the mustard section of the grocery aisle. We run the spectrum from being content with our lives and complacent about searching for birth relatives to being depressed about the "primal wound" of adoption and torn up with identity and belonging issues. And how we think about our adoption can change throughout our lives.

So who, then, is the "ideal adoptee"?

Since our society is caught up with the concept of ideals—ideal climate, weight, job, family size, etc.—it's no surprise that adoptees are also placed on a spectrum.

Think about this for a moment. If you erase an individual's biological profile and legally prevent them from accessing it—something two-thirds of states still do—how does an adoptee evolve into a well-adjusted adult? Does this mean that an adopted person who doesn't seem to be screwed up is the "ideal adoptee"? Or is the adoptee who is seemingly content with the direction of their life and complacent about a search for personal information the "ideal adoptee"?

Much of the adoption-related literature refers to the "well-adjusted adoptee." This person seems satisfied with their role in their adoptive family; does not profess or manifest issues of rejection, loss, identity, or belonging; and does not seem interested in searching out or reuniting with birth relatives. The findings suggest the "well-adjusted adoptee" may have buried or suppressed thoughts and emotions. As the well-adjusted adoptee matures, they are often triggered to question their adoption, and their queries lead to search and reunion. Still, other well-adjusted adoptees do not challenge their adoption in any way.

In the 1950s, my adoptive parents were essentially told this by adoption professionals:

If you love your adopted child—as much as if you'd conceived and carried them for nine months—then they will not question where they came from.

If you raise your adopted child in a heterosexual two-parent household with a strong foundation in religion, and if you establish rules with appropriate rewards and punishment, you will have a well-mannered, well-adjusted child.

Provide your adopted child with adequate explanations in a kind manner and offer support should your child need it.

If you do all this, you will have an "ideal adoptee," a child who will not question their adoption and will not disrupt the family you've put together.

If the "ideal adoptee" is the well-adjusted child who never questions their adoption, I wonder if that adoptee is squashing their desire for knowledge, or if they are simply afraid. Afraid of what their adoptive parents might say and do. Afraid of what they might find during search and reunion, or afraid of how found birth relatives might treat them. Perhaps preserving self-dignity and self-concept, something every person strives to do through life, crafts the well-adjusted adoptee into the "ideal."

It may have seemed to my adoptive parents that I was fine with my adoption, and mostly I was, but keep in mind that I grew up with my twin sister, a factor that sets me apart from most adoptees. When I asked my parents for my adoption paperwork in 2008, I was in my forties and experiencing health issues. My quest for information did not sit well with my adoptive mother, and her lack of support affected our relationship. To her, I had been the well-adjusted adoptee, the ideal, and now I had broken ranks. My probe became more about disrupting the family she'd assembled and less about me and my needs. Her expectations, what she'd been led to believe by the social workers at the time of my adoption, were at odds with my expectations of her as a supportive maternal figure. Such is the dilemma that memoirs are based on.

Did asking questions about my adoption make me less of an ideal adoptee in Mom's eyes? Probably.

From my perspective, questioning my adoption and my subsequent search and reunion with birth relatives made me a well-adjusted person. I acknowledge that adoption search and reunion is not every adoptee's path. I recognize those who choose not to dig into their roots or search for birth relatives are not left of me on the scale of "ideal adoptee." Each of us chooses our path to wholeness. We become our ideal. Worrying about how we stack up against other adoptees or measure up to others' expectations is unhealthy, which is why the notion of "ideal" stinks.

What is ideal? To me, ideal is what is best for the individual and what forms that person into a well-adjusted member of society.

A BREAST BIOPSY LED
TO PERSONAL DISCOVERY

Before I was old enough to know what it meant, my parents informed my twin sister and me that we were adopted. And on several occasions during our formative years, our adoptive parents pulled us into the living room to discuss our closed adoption. During these talks I learned that my folks waited six long years to become parents, how badly they'd "wanted" my twin sister and me, and that they would assist us should we desire more information about our background.

I was a child. And as I listened to my parents' carefully worded speeches, I observed how uneasily they looked from one another to my sister and me. I intuited that my adoption story was "better left alone" and that digging into my closed adoption would upset them. My sister and I had a wonderful childhood. We felt loved and that we belonged. Deferring an adoption probe was an easy decision.

When I was in my late forties, my perspective about "leaving well enough alone" shifted. A suspicious routine mammogram meant I was sent for a biopsy. This incident highlighted what my sister and I couldn't know about our background due to closed adoption. We agreed it was time to search for our birth relatives. Since our parents still possessed our adoption documents, the first step of our search began with them. Dad quickly offered his help, but Mom did little to hide her displeasure. I suspected she feared losing us to our family of origin, and the disruption that our search would impose on the family she and Dad had put together. Nonetheless, I was disturbed that my need for medical information did not alter Mom's attitude. A rift formed between my mother and me.

Due to my twin sister's full-time job, we agreed I would head up the adoption research, but we would split the search costs. The search agency we hired concluded our birth mother had used an alias on our original birth record, the first of many roadblocks. The private investigator I subsequently interviewed referred us to the Confidential Intermediary Service of Illinois. Within a month, a circuit court judge assigned an intermediary to our case, and she gained access to our sealed adoption files. Within weeks the intermediary located an address for our birth mother and sent an outreach letter to her.

Three days shy of our fifty-first birthday, my birth mother returned a short note to the intermediary. She denied my request for present and future contact. Devastated, I appealed to the judge and requested permission to send a second outreach for family health history. Shortly before Mother's Day, my birth mom returned the health questionnaire with the news that one of my six aunts had survived uterine cancer and another was a breast cancer survivor. With these confirmed health risks, my doctors sent me for additional testing.

Nine months after our birth mom denied our request for contact, she phoned the intermediary with questions about the change in Illinois' adoption statutes. The intermediary deftly turned those questions into a request for contact with us. But first our birth mom needed to reveal her secret to the man she had been married to for three decades. After that, we began the arduous exchange of letters and photographs through the intermediary's office. Eventually, this routine progressed to phone calls and then a face-to-face reunion.

In our first in-person get-together, my birth mom handed my sister and me a packet of genealogy and family pictures. Besides French and German heritage, we learned we had Native American heritage. At fifty-two, the freckled and fair-complected woman who stared at me in the mirror each morning finally knew where she came from and why she had been placed for adoption. Despite all this, my adoptive mom wanted no part of the woman who had gifted her with twin daughters.

During that first phone conversation with my birth mom, I quizzed her about my birth father. She faltered when spelling out his last name. Armed with his identity, the intermediary launched another search. Eighteen months later, we were nowhere, and the judge dismissed our case. On a whim, I contacted a genealogist from the town where my birth parents met. Using the information my birth mom had given me, the genealogist discovered my birth dad's true identity. I learned my birth mother had knowingly given us the wrong name. She feared him reentering her life. This lie put our blissful reunion in jeopardy.

With the help of the genealogist and a social worker, I sent a carefully worded letter to the man I now believed was my birth father. The letter I received in return stunned us. Even though my birth dad refused to acknowledge us as his daughters, he attached his family's health history. It revealed that his only sister had died of breast cancer at thirty-nine. Considering this grim fact, his refusal to admit paternity placed us in a conundrum.

After a few days of stewing about my birth dad's letter, the phone rang. The brother I didn't know I had wanted to talk about the father we shared. In that first phone call, we discovered an amazing synchronicity, one that compelled my adoptive mother to shift her perspective. I reveal this happenstance in my memoir, *Twice a Daughter: A Search for Identity, Family, and Belonging (She Writes Press)*. My brother agreed to DNA testing, proving not only that I have Native Americans on both sides of my family but that the threat of breast cancer existed too.

These amazing search outcomes led me to puzzle whether that suspicious mammogram so many years ago was a gift in some strange way. Until my breast biopsy, I believed my adoption was "better left alone," but my health issues forced me to shift that stance. By tracking down my family health history, I discovered outcomes I never expected: I am Native American, and I have a brother and sister eager to be involved in my life.

A breast biopsy not only satisfied my need for personal history but also became the vehicle to clarify issues of identity and belonging and offered the ultimate gift—more family to love.

ADOPTION DAY IS ALMOST LIKE A BIRTHDAY

Because of my closed adoption, there is no record of the events leading up to the births of my twin sister and me. Until I met my birth mom in 2011, I didn't know whether she had seen or held us before surrendering us to the state. So, instead of the play-by-play of what happened on a cold February morning in Chicago, the events surrounding our Adoption Day became the family legend that has trailed us into adulthood. My adoptive family did not celebrate our Adoption Day like adoptees from open adoption currently do—not because it wasn't meaningful, just because it wasn't *a thing* when I was growing up in the 1960s.

When my adoptive parents collected my twin sister and me from St. Vincent's Orphanage in Chicago on March 6, 1959, we were already three weeks old. Information from our adoption file shows that we had been transferred from the hospital to St. Vincent's five days after our births. When my birth mom relinquished her parental rights, we became wards of the state, and The Sisters of Charity—the religious order who ran St. Vincent's—cared for my twin sister and me while we waited for Catholic Charities to place us in a closed adoption.

Sixty years later, my adoptive mother still tears up when she recounts "the call" from Catholic Charities informing her she would become a parent for the first time. Her vivid retelling of this moment has become so real to me; it's almost as if I was in the room with her when she picked up the phone.

Mom had been immersed in a lesson plan with her busy third-grade class at St. Cletus in La Grange. First there was a rap at the classroom door, and then the school secretary stepped inside the classroom.

"You have a phone call in the office," she said.

The entire staff at St. Cletus knew my folks had experienced a half-dozen miscarriages during their five-year marriage. At twenty-six and twenty-seven, Mom and Dad had been waiting nearly two years to adopt.

Mom left the secretary in charge of her class of forty-three students and rushed down the wide hallway. With each hurried step, Mom became more certain the phone call she was about to take was the one that would change her life. When she stopped at the office's open door, she was out of breath. The principal glanced up from the paperwork, looked at my mother's flushed face, and then jabbed a finger toward the school secretary's phone. Mom darted to the adjacent desk, staring at the rotary dial phone with its flashing red "hold" button. She squeezed her eyes shut and sent off a quick prayer, and then she lifted the receiver and punched the blinking red button.

"Hello," she said, her voice soft, questioning.

"Mrs. Ryan? This is Marge Duffy calling, the social worker at Catholic Charities."

"Yes . . . Hello, Marge." Mom moved the phone tighter to her ear.

"Sorry to disturb your school day, Mrs. Ryan, but we have a question about your adoption paperwork."

"Yes . . ."

The corners of Mom's mouth twisted into a frown. She wondered why the social worker had pulled her out of a busy classroom to ask a question that could have been posed in the evening hours.

"In your adoption paperwork, you checked the box next to 'twins.' Did you mean to do that or was it an error?"

Mom remembered putting a neat little checkmark in the box next to "twins," but in all truthfulness she wasn't sure why she had done so. The youngest of twelve, Mom yearned for a big family like the one in which she'd grown up. While declaring that she and Dad would welcome twins had been spontaneous, the decision still felt right.

"Yes, I meant to check the box for twins. It was no mistake." Mom shrugged her shoulders at the waiting principal as if to apologize for the call delaying her return to class.

"Well, in that case, we need to set up a time for you to come to St. Vincent's and pick up your twins, your infant baby girls."

After Mom hung up with the Catholic Charities social worker, the principal and everyone within earshot swarmed around my sobbing mother and helped her dial Dad's office number.

Most adoptees, like me, from the closed adoption era, have no idea what happened on the day we were born. If we're lucky, we can connect with our birth relatives later in life and receive long-desired clues about our birth circumstances. In contrast, today's open adoption experience immediately puts the adopted child in a more transparent situation. The adoption plan establishes a clear flow of information between the birth mother, adoption agency, and adoptive parents. Medical history and genealogy are passed on at the outset. If she chooses, the birth mother plays a role in selecting her child's new parents. Often, the adoptive parents are present for the birth, so they can convey firsthand knowledge of their child's birthday as he/she develops. The child from an open adoption benefits from all this *knowing*. Experts agree that facilitating this knowledge from the outset helps a child form a strong identity and a firm sense of belonging.

Regardless of the type of adoption experience, Adoption Day is a special moment for adoptees and their adoptive parents. Much like a birthday, Adoption Day is about a child being welcomed into the world while commemorating family formation. The important moments and events surrounding Adoption Day bear both celebration and remembering. Acknowledging this unique and precious experience makes the adoptee feel important, validated, and loved.

From the perspective of an adoptee who is both in reunion with birth relatives and maintains a loving, respectful relationship with the adoptive family, I believe what we know about ourselves determines who we become and who we are capable of being.

MY ADOPTION EXPERIENCE INCLUDES BEING A TWIN

When I talk to my twin sister on the phone, it's like listening to my own voicemail recording. Besides sounding alike, we have the same laugh, which begins as a low giggle, then rumbles into a contagious soprano. The similarities don't stop there. Our fine, light-brown hair frames hazel eyes defined by narrow, arched eyebrows. Tall and thin as young girls, we never deviated more than a half inch as we matured. When our adoptive parents received word from Catholic Charities in Chicago that a set of twin girls were waiting for them at St. Vincent's Orphanage, they were informed we were fraternal twins. In 2011, my sister and I learned through genetic testing that we are identical twins.

Besides a strong physical resemblance, my sister and I are like-minded. We share similar habits, interests, opinions, and values. Although fiercely independent, we enjoy being near one another. As children, we shared a bedroom; as young women, we attended the same university; and, as married adults, our homes are a ten-minute drive from one another. Almost always in synch, my twin sister and I don't just get each other—it's as if we are stitched into the same skin.

My sister and I have been together since before we were born and throughout the life that our adoptive parents made for us. That single fact makes being adopted a different equation for us. Like other closed-adoption adoptees, we have always been strongly curious about our biological background, why we were adopted, and which birth relatives we take after physically, intellectually, and emotionally. Going through life with a sibling aligned in looks, thoughts, habits, and deeds, means the sharp edges of adoption has not been razor-sharp.

When I had a breast biopsy in 2008, my twin was in good health, but she was nonetheless immersed in my predicament. My female health issues became the impetus for us to join forces and probe our closed adoption. On the cusp of middle age, we deemed the timing ripe for gathering our truths for ourselves and our children. The right to own our adoption story and health background became a fight that my twin sister and I waged together.

First, Jenny and I plotted how to attain our original birth records and the non-identifying information from our adoption agency's file. After that, we tracked down adoption search choices that were time- and cost-effective. Aligned, we dealt with the concerns and misgivings that our adoptive parents fostered regarding our adoption probe. As we attacked each phase of our search journey, my twin sister and I walked together figuratively hand in hand.

Contacting and connecting with our birth relatives was more complicated than we expected. Because of our bond as twins, we never wavered in our commitment to pursue all avenues until nothing more could be learned. We collaborated, commiserated, and supported each other in the wake of misinformation, lies, disappointment, and rejection. Through all of that, we sustained one another. Likewise, with each adoption search success, we cheered and celebrated together.

Being adopted, searching for birth relatives, and managing reunion are taxing events. More than a decade into the reunion, I doubt I could have endured such a complicated, elongated process had I not sustained such a tight mental and emotional bond with my twin. Because of my involvement in a post-adoption support group, I'm aware this luxury—searching for biological relatives alongside a full sibling—is not possible for most adoptees.

Just as I cannot know what it's like not to be adopted, I can't comprehend what my life would be like without my twin sister. Both are at the core of my identity, melded and fused. I will be forever grateful to Catholic Charities for implementing an adoption policy that refused to separate children from a multiple birth. Growing up with my twin sister is the greatest blessing resulting from my closed adoption.

THREE THINGS ADOPTEES WONDER

The decision to look for my biological relatives was driven by suspicious mammograms and a biopsy. Besides the need for medical history, that frightening scenario became the impetus for acting on latent desires: *who am I, where did I come from*, and *why was I adopted*. As I assembled the tools to dig into my personal story, I read voraciously about adoption and the adoption triad. It was in this research that I realized those three questions—who, where, and why—were common among adoptees; pondering them was normal and essential in forming a sense of self.

I can't remember a time when I hadn't known I was adopted. The oldest of six, I wasn't the only child in my family that was adopted. My twin sister and I were adopted first, then two years later my brother. After us, my parents were gifted with three biological children. We were a hodgepodge of human beings: three brunettes, a redhead, and two blonds. Some of us were tall, skinny, and freckly, and others were average height and stocky. Solid parents and consistent parenting molded the six of us into a family. When I think about this now, the fact that I was one of the adopted kids didn't seem like a big deal. Like grabbing a towel after a shower, it's what you do. It's what you are. It's the way of your life.

I was happy in the family into which I was adopted. I felt loved and wanted. I was given many opportunities, took advantage of those, and relished in making my parents proud. While I admit that I had always been curious about my birth circumstances, I did not possess the courage to voice this aloud. At bedtime, my mind wandered to those uncertainties: *who am I, where did I come from,* and *why was I adopted.* I picked up those three thoughts like they were stones on the beach. I studied them, tossed them around, and then the sheep I counted chased them away.

You would have thought that my twin and I would've talked about "the big three," the doubts that niggled our adopted id and ego. If we did, I don't recall the conversation. Perhaps we didn't have to. As identical twins we intuit a lot through looks and glances. Our relationship has always been deep without the need for cumbersome conversation. If we didn't talk about these adoption questions, our brains coped with them. I also don't recall saying to my friends or parents: I want to know who I was before, where I came from, and why I was adopted. If I had uttered those statements, it would have implied that I wanted to get at those questions, and it would indicate that I was unhappy with my life. That was not the case with my adoption. I was content with my circumstances.

In my formative years, my adoptive parents would periodically bring up the subject of my adoption, asking if I wanted to seek out information. It was like they took out an adoption thermometer to see where my temperature had risen on the subject. Those were uncomfortable moments. "No, I'm fine" was my standard reply. At that stage in my life, I was fine not knowing the details of my adoption, but those pesky bedtime thoughts persisted.

Then at forty-eight, I wasn't fine. My health was threatened. One of the hardest calls I had to make was to my folks asking for my adoption papers. I needed not only their help but also their support. While my mom and dad supported an adoption probe in theory, when they handed over the files, I saw fear, sadness, and disappointment in their eyes. My health was threatened, and their sense of family was in jeopardy. I assured them: I would never call anyone else Mom and Dad.

So where do I come out on all of this? "Who I am" is the product of four people I consider my parents. They all made me who I am, and my heart is big enough to include each of them. "Where I came from" incorporates where I grew up and the rich history of my biological ancestors. I am proud to know that I am of French and German, Scottish-Irish, and Chippewa descent. These facts allow me to be what is truly in me rather than what adoption told me I was.

The answer to "why I was adopted" was the trickiest. On one level I know that I am from a relationship that didn't work, I had educated parents, and they were not teenagers. Through counseling I've learned my birth parents' choices were not about rejecting me personally. Yet, I still have work to do in accepting some of the "why" of what was revealed during my searches and reunions.

Years have evaporated since my folks handed over the adoption paperwork. I am still in reunion with my birth mother and two siblings from my father's first marriage. My birth father died suddenly, and I was not given the opportunity to meet him. I am inordinately grateful to have found so much family to love. Every day is richer because they are in my life.

Launching my adoption probe was not easy, nor was the battle for a full medical background and pedigree. Now healthy,

I can say the breast biopsy turned out to be the key to answering questions I avoided for years. It is a relief to have wrestled the questions and assimilated the answers. I sleep better now that the sheep have chased the questions away for good.

THREE IDENTICAL STRANGERS

When the documentary *Three Identical Strangers* premiered at the Sundance Film Festival in 2018, I was not just interested in the story. I was invested in it. Directed by Tim Wardle, the film touches on medical ethics, the nature versus nurture debate, and the issue of multiple birth siblings separated by adoption. The story begins in 1980 when two nineteen-year-old boys discover purely by accident that they are identical brothers adopted by different families. The tale grows more complex when a third brother surfaces; the young men discover they are identical triplets separated at birth. The trio hits the talk-show circuit, and their lives intertwine. Life is glorious for them, and then it isn't.

In the late 1950s, my twin sister and I were placed for adoption through Catholic Charities in Chicago. Unlike the New York–based Louise Wise adoption agency that handled the triplets' adoptions, Catholic Charities has a strict policy of placing children from a multiples-pregnancy together. The Louise Wise adoption agency separated the triplets in this story, and they had a history of doing so in other cases. The organization was in cahoots with Dr. Peter Neubauer, a prominent psychologist who wished to study nature versus nurture. Much like the documentary's viewing population, I found this outcome unfathomable, unconscionable, and immoral.

Inherent in the adoption experience are a multitude of issues. Identity, self-worth, belonging, trauma, attachment disorder, and rejection head the list. Throughout their formative years, adoptees spend much energy considering how they fit in with their adoptive families, how they stack up in society, and when and if they will launch a search into their adoption.

If you have a twin or triplet by your side as you address adoption's complexities, you have a good chance of hitting adulthood with only a handful of scars. However, if you add to the injustices inherent in adoption by introducing another variable—being separated from your identical sibling(s)—you have created a toxic cocktail that affects development and future relationships. A fundamental coping mechanism has essentially been removed and eliminated. One would ask why handicap the already handicapped.

My twin sister has always been my go-to friend, fellow problem-solver, troublemaker, and confidante. Her presence settled me when I was stressed, supported me when I struggled, and cheered me when I succeeded. I am not me without her, and vice versa. Depriving multiple-birth siblings of daily contact with their alter egos effectively throws them off balance for life. It is messing with nature. The fact that this documentary is a true story, a crime perpetuated by a psychologist and an adoption agency, is deeply troubling. Their collaboration and complicity are criminal.

As an adoptee and identical twin, I found that this film brought forward emotions and thoughts long after I left the screening. First, I felt fortunate adoption had not separated me from my twin. I pulsed with the injustice of these young men being denied the solace of their sibling bonds throughout infancy and adolescence. And I identified with the insurmountable joy of finding an unknown sibling. When I was in my fifties, I connected with a half-brother and sister, and we are still in reunion. As grateful as I was to be welcomed into my siblings' families, I resented every gatekeeper who had prevented my contact with them.

Kudos to the investigative journalist who pursued the story of the *Three Identical Strangers*, the film crew who brought it to the screen, and all who made possible the justice for these men that followed, albeit late in the game. I admire the courage of the two brothers who allowed their story to be told and presented.

Three Identical Strangers was difficult for me to view—not because I'm an adoptee and a twin, but because there is no way to right the wrong for these men. Separating siblings through adoption for scientific and psychological study is morally and ethically wrong. This film is not just a must-see for those familiar with the adoption experience. It is important to every socially conscious and responsible adult.

MY CHILDHOOD FANTASIES
CENTERED ON ADOPTION

When I was a young girl, before I turned sixteen and was awarded a room of my own, I would lie in bed at night and squint across the crevasse of lime green shag toward my twin sister's matching canopy bed. I watched her sink into the early stages of sleep, her chest heaving ever so slightly. The sighs she whispered were from our day at an over-chlorinated pool, a mile-long bike ride, and too much candy from the five-and-dime. Her shaggy braids and willowy bangs dusted the pillow; her tummy warmed the white cotton sheets; one long, narrow foot escaped the white eyelet comforter, her perfect toes pointed as if hurling an accusation at the thick, gnarly carpet.

This roommate, my twin sister, I knew nearly as well as I knew myself. I knew what her reactions would be seconds before she reacted, her moods before they lifted or plummeted, and her temperament before it broiled or soured. Her shy smile meant she was annoyed or waiting. I appreciated what would make her laugh, her head turn, her eyes roll. I knew what she and I would save to talk about when we could be alone in our bedroom with the matching canopy beds and green carpet. Because I knew all this about my sister, I suspected she too indulged in fantasies before she drifted off: fantasies about the parents who gave us up, placed us for adoption, and were still "out there."

As I studied my sleeping womb-mate, I let myself invent lives for our other set of parents. I imagined them as the cool people I looked up to in my limited childhood world. I was certain our birth mother was one of those hot, popular girls, a cheerleader headed off to a good college who snagged the dreamy, sweet physical specimen on the football or basketball team. Their relationship, admired and coveted by their peers, was too intense for their age, resulted in the making of not one but two "mini me's."

Convinced of this scenario, I imagined my birth parents heading off to college or careers while my twin and I were adopted by folks desperate for an instant family.

In retrospect, I must have heard this scenario somewhere in the news, or read about it, because these were not suggestions made by my adoptive parents or facts disseminated by the adoption agency. These were fantasies, ideas that made me feel better or gave structure to the wonder about why two beautiful girls would be gifted to another family to raise.

My pre-slumber musings took several tracks, an elaborate trail of paths that I picked up randomly when the house was still, the day was done, my twin slept, and my mind allowed me to consider what might have been. There was the who-were-these-people route, as I mentioned above. I never considered anything but the cute cheerleader/star-stud scenario. Mostly, my pre-teen mind prevented me from going down the one-night stand, married-male-boss-female-secretary/assistant, rape, or incest rabbit holes. I liked the idea of a passionate young couple at the top of the heap, copulating and making my twin and me. These fantasies satisfied the answer to the question: Why was I adopted?

The question did not haunt me. It nagged. Nagged like homework on Sunday night, like dishes in the sink, like a burned-out light bulb. The mystery of my birth parents pestered me when I studied my kids, wondering where they got the freckles, the thick limbs and athletic prowess to play college sports. It hassled me when I had a breast biopsy, my uterine fibroid flared, and my colonoscopy showed polyps. And when I turned fifty years old, I resolved to get the monkey off my back.

I got lucky. The same year I decided to search for my birth relatives, Illinois' adoption statutes changed. I was given access to my original birth record. The information led me down several difficult paths, but after intense sleuthing I discovered my truths. My existence was not a result of a coupling between a cheerleader and a football star. Instead, two twenty-something consenting adults, elementary school teachers, who couldn't agree on religion or marriage, launched my life. It took me weeks to assimilate the truths and let go of the more pleasing fantasy.

My pre-teen brain dithered with other fantasies when sleep failed. Like other adoptees, I wondered *will they come back for me* and *what are they doing now.* I assumed, hoped, and expected that my first set of parents worried about whether my twin and I were happy, whether we were adjusting well to our new families and if we were healthy and well cared for. I wanted my biological parents to worry about these things. I expected they did, and I wondered whether they would return to find my sister and me.

That's as far as my young mind allowed me to wander. I don't recall worrying about their potential visit, whether they'd attempt to reclaim us, or whether I would have to choose to go with them or stay with my adopted family. That's the thing about fantasy; your mind only goes where it is pleasurable to wander. True musing doesn't deal with conflict; that is what nightmares are for.

ADD FAMILY REUNIONS
TO THE LIST OF TRIGGERS

Several events or circumstances usher in an adoptee's anxiety and frustration. Occasions like birthdays, Mother's Day, Father's Day, and, of course, the holiday season can trigger feelings of abandonment, rejection, loss, and trauma in an adoptee. Trips to the doctor can be problematic, for it is in this clinical setting that an adoptee confronts a major shortcoming: the lack of some or all of the birth family's medical history. To the adult adoptee, this failure to produce health documentation is frustrating and embarrassing; the experience often leads to adoption anger.

Add family reunions to the adopted person's touch list.

My adoptive father's family was small enough that Thanksgiving, Christmas, and Easter sufficed and supplanted organized family reunions. Over my formative years, I grew close to some of these cousins, and I value their role in my life. My adoptive mom was the youngest of thirteen. Each of her siblings produced an average of six kids, which means on her side I can claim scores of first cousins.

Until the reunion process became unwieldy, my mother's family gathered at a picnic grove in the summertime. Games, prizes, face painting, hot dogs, and hamburgers. Sounds fun, right? On the surface, any child should have a blast at these fun-filled affairs. When I returned from these events, I lay exhausted, sunburned, and bug-bitten in bed. I did have fun, but something troubled me. It wasn't until I was a teenager noodling in a spiral-bound journal that I figured out what undermined the fun of family reunions.

Here's the thing. When an adoptee heads off to a family reunion, they know the event is a get-together for their adoptive family's biological relatives. As a legal member of the adoptive family, the adoptee knows they belong to this multi-generational group. However, even if an adoptee is welcomed and encouraged to take part in the reunion activities, we are cognizant of what is missing—we lack the basic biology that ties us to these folks. Even though we may want to connect, something feels off.

Let me put it another way. The adopted person knows that somewhere out there, in some other picnic grove, another family reunion is taking place—one that their genes gave them a ticket to attend, but that ticket got taken away.

Whenever we have reason to gather, I enjoy visiting with the cousins in my adoptive family. The occasional wedding or baby shower used to pull us together, but sadly funerals and memorials force our reunions lately. Over the past fifty years, I've grown used to these aunts, uncles, and cousins. And they are comfortable with me. We know our way around one another. Even though we don't have genes that link us, we have shared experiences that bind us. I care about these folks, and it doesn't matter to me that we don't match on 23andMe. I value them as people who played a role in my life. I want and need them in my life. And I am grateful for their inclusiveness.

When I connected with my birth mother in 2011, she shared genealogical data and scores of photos. As we sat in her front parlor, my birth mom offered an oral history about these relatives. The pictures came to life for me. My people. Blood relatives. My biological kin. It thrilled me to match the biographies my mother shared with the folks I'd found on the genealogical sites. I was not just interested in these biological strangers; I was captivated. I wanted to get to know them.

Because she was a scorned and shamed unwed mother from the 1950s, it was no surprise that my birth mother took her time telling her extended family about the two daughters who had come back into her life. I was patient with her while she went through this process. I wept for her as she agonized over how and when to disclose her shocking secret. I cheered for her when she succeeded. And I was equally glad when the news was well received. This was a benchmark that I was certain would lead to introductions.

Every year in a picnic grove several states away, my birth mother, her siblings, and other living relatives gather for a potluck reunion. Every year, she sends me photos of the reunion, taking great pains to label each person in her neat schoolteacher script. As of this writing, we are more than a decade into our burgeoning relationship as mother and daughter. Not once have I been invited to attend these reunions. It's a one-way mirror. I can look in from afar but have yet to be asked into the inner circle.

I belong but I don't.

In my head, I know that my genes afford me a legitimate reason to be included, but it is easier for my birth mom for me to stay at home. I accept the situation, but the reality stings. I wish that I could have my cake and eat it too. As I reflect on family reunions, I wish I shared more than simply good times with my adoptive cousins and that my biological family was more inclusive.

THE HOLIDAYS CAN BE
A TIPPING POINT

The holidays are a special time of year. For many people they are also a tipping point.

A mere glance at holiday lights and decorations ushers in nostalgia. We miss the people that won't be able to gather with us. So, too, we feel bad about the gifts we wanted to buy but couldn't because they were backordered, discontinued, or out of our price range. Nostalgia, longing, and regret can shepherd in other emotions. Suppressed feelings like inadequacy, vulnerability, and loneliness often pierce the joy we want to feel during this special time of year.

For many adoptees, the loss and rejection inherent in the adoption experience surface during the holidays. These feelings are understandable given that the Christmas story is centered on the gift of a child—a child born in unseemly circumstances but welcomed first by kings and then acknowledged by centuries of people. The adopted child/adult, however content he or she is with life in their adoptive family, knows another set of parents decided not to include them in their family. As an adoptee, I know the pain of glancing around the holiday table and noting who is not seated there among the people I call my "loved ones."

Because of this "primal wound" inherent in adoption, many adoptees struggle with identity and belonging. The holidays further remind us of who we belong to and who we do not. As more and more states address the need to overhaul antiquated adoption laws, adult adoptees are locked in court battles to gain access to basic medical history and genealogy. If an adoptee is fortunate to have the proper information to reach out to birth relatives, many struggle to connect and be acknowledged. Some adoptees know the pain of being dismissed by a biological parent and are warned never to reach out again. For an adoptee, the season of joy can be another reminder of all that adoption took from them.

It's safe to say that 2020 was a tipping point for many people across the globe. Loss and rejection are not specific to any group of people. Disappointment, trauma, and loss were the unwelcome themes of 2020, a year aptly nicknamed "the year like no other."

Many experts share tips for coping with the stress of the holidays. The Mayo Clinic offers this advice: Acknowledge your feelings—it's normal to feel sadness and grief; reach out for support if you feel lonely or isolated; be realistic about expectations and open to creating new traditions; set aside differences and accept family members and friends for who they are.

And if you are an adoptee disconnected from your family of origin, seek counsel to better cope with the stress that the holidays trigger. Perhaps this is the year you launch an adoption search. Or it may be the time you decide you are content with your situation and that "leaving well enough alone" is the right choice for you.

WHY NOW, WHY WAIT,
AND WHY NOT?

One of the items I was coached to include in the first letter to my birth mother was why I was searching for her at this point in our lives.

As she opened my outreach letter—handwritten pages that landed in her mailbox out of the blue—she might wonder, "Why now?" I addressed this concern in the opening paragraph of my letter: I'm searching for you now because I have a medical concern and would like my family's medical history.

My search for information was complicated and stretched over many years. Within a year of locating my *first* mother, she provided a full health history and complete pedigree. Eighteen months after I entered a full reunion with her, the genealogist I hired finally tracked down my birth dad. While he did not agree to meet with me, my biological father complied with my request for family medical history.

As I shared the details of my midlife project—searching for my family of origin—with friends and extended family we quickly moved past the "why now?" question to a different one. Why did I wait to search, and why do many adoptees delay researching their adoption until later in life?

An adult adoptee might postpone their research in deference or loyalty to their adoptive family. I have several adult adoptee friends who decided to wait until their adoptive parents had died before digging into their adoption history. They claim they did so out of respect and gratitude for the life that had been provided to them.

Often what drives an adoption search is the fear that if one waits too long, the birth parents will not be alive to pass on vital details and family history. Still other adoptees are driven to dig for their personal stories before they are legally adults; they believe that they have the "right to information," and they should own it. A limiting factor is the laws of the state in which the adoption was legalized, and whether the adoption was closed, private, or open.

"Why not?"—or why don't all adoptees search—makes up the last contingent. An adoptee who doesn't search for birth relatives might be content with the course of their life and unwilling to risk damaging relationships with the family who they have come to love and know best. Adoptees delay searching because their adoptive parents are still alive or feel that a search opens a world of trouble. Many believe that if their birth parents wanted them, they wouldn't have placed them for adoption, and that it is too late to connect with their birth relatives. Still others consider the cost of searching and realize that they do not have the resources to do so. And all adoptees fear rejection or the facts that will come to light. With so many reasons not to search for birth relatives, it is not surprising that many adoptees ignore their beginnings and lead the life chosen for them.

In closing, many questions factor into the viability of adoption search and reunion. *Why now, why wait,* and *why not* are the most prevalent concerns that pop up as adoptees, adoptive parents, and birth relatives navigate the tricky realm of the adoption experience. Each question should be considered and discerned before launching into a decision that changes lives.

While I am content with having found the answers I sought at a critical juncture in my adult life, each adult adoptee or birth parent must chart their own path regarding search and reunion.

WHAT'S ON YOUR OBR?

Recently, one of my children needed a certified original birth record (OBR) as proof to some government agency that they were who they purported to be. As the matriarch of my family, I am the keeper of all things important.

I scoured my desk for the fat red file labeled "Important Papers." Tattered and smudged from over thirty years of use, it bulges under a thick rubber band in a hanging file drawer. Jammed with social security info, birth certificates, baptismal records, and yellowed envelopes with snippets of hair from first haircuts, the thick file also holds army discharge papers and marriage certificates. From deep within the stack of paperwork, I unearthed the certified birth record in question, made a copy for myself, and then sent the original off to my child.

Before sliding the red folder back into the waiting slot in the file cabinet, I dug out my own birth certificate. Because of my adoption, I have two birth records. I keep them paper-clipped together like twins—though closely related, they are not identical. Both documents are important, but the one clipped in front is the birth record my parents received when my adoption was finalized months after they'd picked us up from the orphanage. While entirely legal, this birth record is redacted, meaning most of the original details were purged and revised per the 1950s Illinois adoption statutes.

Have you ever considered the details on your OBR?

Not often is my guess. Most folks only glance at their birth record when renewing their driver's license. However, if you are an adoptee from the closed adoption era, you have scrutinized your redacted birth certificate. Often. And each time you studied it, you wished your truths would magically appear like a scratch-off lottery ticket. Of most interest to adoptees are the boxes where our parental names appear. There are other interesting boxes on the OBR, like the hospital where the birth was recorded, birth weight and height, and the doctor's name attesting to the live birth. There's also a square for multiple births. A checkmark in the small box labeled "Twin1" reminds me that I was born before my sister.

All these details are somewhat boring unless some are missing, left blank, or redacted. On an adoptee's redacted OBR, the birth parents' names and places of origin are replaced with our adoptive parents' details. The department for vital records in most states will not release any of the biological parents' data unless requested by the adoptee and only if the current adoption statutes provide for the release. I petitioned the state of Illinois when the adoption law changed in 2011 for my OBR.

Here's the irony. The name in the box above "mother" is not my birth mother's real name. The custom at the time was to encourage birth mothers to take an alias to protect their privacy. This was legal in those days. Unlike some adoptees, I couldn't use my original birth record to locate my birth mother. I needed the Illinois Confidential Intermediary Service, an organization operating under a judge's court order, to access Catholic Charities' sealed records and obtain my birth mother's identity.

I received my OBR in November 2011, but I was disappointed not to learn my birth father's name. In the space marked "father" were the words *Legally Omitted*. He had been "legally omitted" because my birth mother was not required to disclose his name per 1950s adoption laws. It was astounding to learn that my first birth certificate, my OBR, comprised an alias and a non-entity. Current adoption law dictates that birth fathers must acknowledge and explicitly sign away their parental rights, just as has always been required of birth mothers.

Before returning the red "Important Papers" file to my desk drawer, I sorted the paperwork and popped all of it into a crisp, new manila folder. My two OBRs are clipped together at the front for easy reference. I've grown fond of perusing my paperwork and feel comfortable with both my birth name and my adoptive name. I received these sets of names in the first year of my life, and each was gifted to me by different parents. Possessing the identities that would have appeared on an unredacted record of my birth and adoption was not a seamless journey. Success was often in doubt, but what matters most is that by attaining my original birth record and by accessing my sealed adoption records, I now know all of who I am.

LONG-TERM EFFECTS OF A
REDACTED OBR

In the previous essay, I shared that "Legally Omitted" appeared in the space on my original birth record where my birth father's name should've been. For me, lacking my birth father's name meant three things. First, I had to locate my birth mother. If I could find her, then I would ask for his name. While I was hopeful, I knew this was too much to expect. Finding my birth mom was one thing. Expecting her to recall and share my birth dad's identity was something else entirely. From my readings and research, I knew this could prove problematic.

Here's what happened. After my birth mom first denied contact with me, I waited nearly eight months for her to change her mind. In our first phone call, I mustered up the nerve to ask her how she had met my birth dad, then I asked for his name. She hesitated as if puzzling over the spelling. Eventually she offered it up, and some identifying information that would come in handy later.

The search for my biological father languished for over a year. I wasn't sure whether my birth mom had remembered his name incorrectly or if she had lied. Thanks to the tenacity of a genealogist in Minnesota, his correct identity was eventually unearthed. Later, I learned my birth mom lied because she did not want him re-entering her life. My birth dad died without acknowledging me as his child, but my half siblings readily welcomed my twin and me into their lives.

One of the most startling discoveries I made about my new family is our Native American heritage. Learning about our Chippewa ancestors has felt like one of those television ads for Ancestry.com. Being Native American had never been on my radar. I have light brown hair, fair skin, freckles, and hazel eyes. My looks scream Scottish-Irish or Danish, both of which also appeared on my ethnic pie chart.

Thanks to my new siblings, I became privy to a myriad of details relating to our Native American lineage. We descend from a union between a Canadian Chippewa princess and a Scottish-Irish fur trader. Together, these ancestors produced a slew of sturdy folk who settled in northern Minnesota; their names appear in state history books. The more I read about my heritage, the more I became curious about how I might connect with the Chippewa from northern Minnesota. I investigated the requirements to be considered a member of the Chippewa tribe.

As mentioned, my birth father's name does not appear on my birth record. I discovered that for me to be considered a bona fide Chippewa, his name had to appear on my original birth record. My inability to be recognized as a Chippewa isn't the biggest heartache I've ever faced, but I am disappointed. It is hard to identify with a group when they refuse you membership.

The long-term effects of the mistruths on OBRs of adoptees from the closed adoption era are far-reaching. Isn't it a shame that adoptees, like me, can't claim our heritage because of the decisions made by adoption gatekeepers?

It's time to reverse those errors.

DOCUMENTS OFTEN REVEAL
NEW PUZZLES

During the years I probed my closed adoption, besides search angels, statutes, and gatekeepers, I encountered periods of interminable waiting. Limbo bookended every step I made. The time between asking for help and getting a reply varied wildly. The norm was for days to fold into weeks, and those weeks frequently slipped into months. On one occasion, however, my query was immediately answered, and its result posed new puzzles.

Pasted in the beginning pages of my baby book is a handmade christening announcement. The heavy white card stock bears writing in silver ink by my adoptive mother's careful hand. Baptism is the first sacrament a child receives in the Catholic faith. The custom is to baptize an infant as soon as possible, to erase "the original sin" passed on by Adam and Eve, so if a baby dies their unmarred soul can enter the kingdom of heaven.

The pages following my christening notice are littered with miscellany, basic baby physical descriptions and habits. Conspicuously absent are my baptismal certificate and snapshots commemorating the event. Adopted through Catholic Charities, I'd been told my baptism occurred at Holy Name Cathedral in Chicago.

Instead of asking my adoptive mom what happened to my baptismal certificate, I called the rectory at Holy Name Cathedral. Situated on North State Street, Holy Name Cathedral is the seat of the Archdiocese of Chicago. Any sacrament received in the Cathedral is an honor reserved strictly for parishioners. St. Vincent's, the orphanage from which I was adopted, is a few blocks south of Holy Name. Technically that makes my orphanage part of the Holy Name Parish. It made perfect sense to me that St. Vincent's babies would receive their first sacrament at the cathedral.

In calling the rectory at Holy Name, I planned to request a copy of my baptismal certificate, then inquire what other information about me resided in their files. As I lingered on hold while the administrator checked the baptismal records, I imagined the woman flipping through dusty tomes in the rectory basement to get to February 1959, her bifocals scrolling down the names that began with "R." The longer I held, I could almost see the line where my given name popped up, handwritten in an elegant cursive beside my baptismal date, birthdate, and adoptive parents' names.

"I have located the records," the woman said in a rushed manner. "I will mail you a copy in the morning."

Before I could think about it, words sprayed out. "I was adopted from St. Vincent's. Are my birth parents' names written there?"

"We would never have received that information. When an infant was adopted, the paperwork was sent over to us from St. Vincent's. At this office we would have entered the baptismal date, and then the adoptive parents' names would be entered alongside the infant's new given name. That's all that is listed here. No birth names. No birth parents' names."

Something in her statement puzzled me. I asked, "What is the date of my baptism at Holy Name?"

"You were not baptized at the cathedral. You received your first sacrament at St. Vincent's. In the chapel. It was important to baptize babies as soon as possible. Nurses acted as stand-in godparents. This office only certified the sacrament." She finished by giving me my baptismal date, which I hadn't realized coincided with my adoptive mother's birthday.

Somehow, I stumbled through a courteous thank-you and the recitation of my mailing address.

Astounded that a simple request for a copy of a document had yielded two new pieces of information, I decided to call my mother.

At some point in my formative years, my adoptive mother might have explained she hadn't been present at my baptism, and in fact neither had my adoptive father or godparents. But she hadn't. For my adoptive mom, the point was not whose arms held me as the sacred chrism was poured over my forehead, but that I'd already been blessed and free of sin.

While the solution to my dilemma—where was my baptismal certificate—had been easily solved, other puzzling questions emerged. Over the course of figuring out my story this past decade, I've discovered family secrets are stubborn and unwieldy. While acquiring a document may seem simple, what it unearths has a ripple effect.

I doubt I will ever be patient about waiting for information to land in my inbox. And it is quite likely that I will be skeptical about the veracity of all the details I receive.

I FEEL LIKE A FAKE

Imposter syndrome is the fear of being "found out" or discovered that you are not who you pretend to be, or not as competent as you have presented yourself. People suffering from imposter syndrome express feelings of anxiety, stress, or depression. They have thoughts such as *I must not fail, I feel like a fake,* and *I'm just lucky.* Early research in this area showed women profoundly identified with this phenomenon, yet follow-up studies proved men experienced it as well.

As both a female and an adoptee, I have at times felt like an imposter. There were moments when I was conscious of saying to myself, "I must not fail. I feel like a fake. I just got lucky."

Other adoptees have expressed having bouts of imposter syndrome. It stems from the notion that the identity which we are currently using is not our original persona. In a sense, adoptees live under an alias, a fake or assumed name selected by well-meaning adults, our adoptive parents. The point is that adoptees are not the people they started to be when the sperm hit the egg. After labor and delivery, we ceased to be who nature had intended and we became someone else: our adoptive parents' pride and joy.

Adoptees are aware the life we were genetically meant to have is not the one we are living. (Whether the life an adoptee leads *is* the one they were *meant to* have is another essay.) To be an adoptee means living an existence of duality. An assumed identity replaces the original and is validated when adoption is certified. The adoptee's redacted birth record becomes the new passport for a lifetime.

Besides the name change, how else might an adoptee feel like an imposter?

Let me offer an example from my life. Chicago is made up of ethnic neighborhoods: Polish, Irish, Italian, Greek, and so on. My adoptive father was raised as an Irish Catholic and so was my adoptive mom. With no known heritage, I assumed my adoptive parents'. Thrust into Chicago's Irish culture, my sister and I were indoctrinated into Irish festivals and customs. We attended the city's St. Patrick's Day parades, listened to Irish music, laughed at Irish jokes, and memorized its folklore.

With my dark hair, fair freckled skin, and greenish eyes, in my youth I passed easily for an Irish lass. As a high schooler, I entered the St. Patrick's Day Parade Queen contest. Honored to be a member of the court, I rode atop a convertible and finessed my "queen wave." In college, I represented the city of Chicago at the Rose of Tralee festival in Ireland. Proud to look Irish and be recognized as such, inwardly I doubted. I doubted and I doubted. Was the blood in my veins Gaelic, or was I an imposter, a fake, a liar? Had I cheated a true Irish lass out of her due honor? You can imagine my relief in 2011 when DNA analysis showed that half of my ethnic background was Scottish-Irish.

For nearly forty years, adoptee imposter syndrome colored how I thought about myself. Learning the truth about my heritage healed my inner doubts. It's too bad that closed adoption could not reveal my true heritage long before I became a middle-aged woman.

CLEANING OUT THE BASEMENT INFLUENCED MY WRITING JOURNEY

As a young girl, I was devoted to my journals.

The spiral-bound notebooks I selected held bright, psychedelic covers unlike the Mead variety I filled for my classes at school. Like most teens, I wrote about family life, friends, and hobbies, but many of my journal entries centered on my closed adoption. Between the ruled lines, I shared what I thought about as an adoptee and how I wished I knew more about my background.

When I went to college, I stashed the journals in the bottom of a sturdy cardboard box and covered them carefully with wrapped keepsakes. I sealed the box with nearly an entire roll of masking tape and marked it "Julie—High School." Then I stowed the carton in an obscure corner of my parents' basement.

Fast-forward thirty years.

At forty-eight years old, I was sent for a breast biopsy. This nervewracking experience compelled my twin sister and me to get serious about learning what medical conditions ran in our bloodline. When our adoption search stretched from months into years, I picked up my old habit: journaling. As I recorded the crazy twists and turns of my adoption probe, I began to toy with the idea of writing a book.

Yet, composing such a personal narrative under my real name made me uncomfortable. So, I dabbled with the idea of a pen name; my birth name became a consideration. During the five years it took to locate my birth relatives, I created several drafts of my search story. Concurrently, I enrolled in courses through the Writer's Studio at the University of Chicago. And as I studied the tools of my craft, I realized the chapters I had written lacked compelling characters, riveting scenes, gripping dialogue, and a definitive story arc. Frustrated, I set aside the memoir and turned to the genre I loved to read: fiction.

For months I worked on conjuring a story world rife with believable characters and an intriguing plot. The novel I chose to write was influenced by my experience as an adoptee working with a confidential intermediary whose job was contacting birth relatives. Even though I used a fictitious plot with made-up characters, I still wrote about what I knew. I grew more and more excited about my novel's progress and promise. But as often happens, real life interfered, and the completion of my novel hit a speed bump.

My husband and I decided it was time to downsize from the suburban home where we'd raised our family. Clearing out that big old Victorian consumed months of my time, leaving me little time to write. I was forever sorting, donating, and reselling unwanted household items. Not surprisingly, I had saved one of the most onerous tasks for last: organizing the storage area in our antiquated basement. Yet, this final chore provided a bonus, one that changed the course of my writing career.

On one of the lower shelves, behind the dust-encrusted bins of Christmas ornaments and kids' memorabilia, a dilapidated, heavily taped box marked "Julie—High School" appeared. I yanked it from the shelving. As I stripped away the old tape, I grinned. Rummaging through the contents, I discovered my old journals hidden at the bottom. I filled my arms with the old notebooks and plopped on the staircase to read.

Journal after journal, I scanned entries penned in a familiar yet foreign hand. The narrative voice was young but also tender, honest, and endearing. While my adolescent musings lacked scenic details and dialogue, the young author's voice was intuitive, reliable, and captivating. Holding the journals to my chest, I charged up the stairs and stashed the found treasure in a box marked "Important Documents—Hand move." When I returned to the chaos in the storage room, a plan crystallized: Shelve the novel for the time being and, using the journals, refocus on writing the memoir about my search for birth relatives.

As I considered reprioritizing my writing projects, I realized somewhere along the way my goals had shifted. Revealing personal moments no longer felt awkward. Hiding behind a pseudonym didn't feel right either. And by sharing the details of my real-life adoption search, I believed other adoptees might benefit from the mistakes I'd made and from what I learned. Suddenly, my writing had a higher purpose than telling a story. I felt a sense of urgency to get my story down so I could share, inspire, and inform.

Armed with my journals and the outline of my adoption search saga, I imposed the elements of fiction I'd learned from coursework into my tale. I strove to make my characters appealing yet relatable. I infused pivotal scenes with rich sensory detail, and I added necessary dialogue. The boring narrative I'd penned several years before sprang to life. But for my memoir to shine and be true to its genre, it needed carefully placed reflection from me, the narrator. That's where the journaling work I had done throughout my life came into play.

In May 2021, my debut memoir, *Twice a Daughter: A Search for Identity, Family, and Belonging*, released. I began writing my story a decade before that, sidelined it briefly to pen a novel, and then returned to the original manuscript with the required skills to serve its needs. As much as I love blogging, crafting personal essays, and memoir, when the time is right the unfinished novel will make its way out of the desk drawer. One of the things I've gleaned from more experienced writers is to repurpose and reuse discarded writing.

It's a shame to let ideas and good words go to waste.

WHEN MY LIFE TOOK A DIFFERENT
DIRECTION THAN I'D PLANNED

In the closing chapters of Michelle Obama's autobiography, *Becoming,* she reflects upon the moment her life swerved. She stepped out of the corporate legal arena at Sidley and Austen, took a pay cut, and entered the not-for-profit world. Obama claims the shift she made from corporate to private and her efforts in that arena influenced her choices when she became First Lady. As I finished her book, I reflected upon the times my life took a different direction than I'd planned. Like Obama, several experiences led me to that proverbial fork in the road. And like the First Lady, I offer a long reply to a seemingly simple question.

At sixteen, immersed in a high-school midterm, I was summoned to the principal's office. There, I met up with my twin sister and younger brother. Without any explanation, the school secretary sent us all home. In the middle of the school day. In the middle of midterm exams. No reason given. For the twenty-minute ride home, the three of us barely spoke. As I gazed out the car window, I knew something must be wrong at home.

Suffering from a chest cold, our youngest sister—age four and one of my adoptive parents' three biological children—had stopped breathing. The ER docs were unable to save her. Following my sister's sudden death, my family became dysfunctional. My father immersed himself in work. Instead of seeking grief therapy, Mom sipped wine in the afternoons with the neighbor ladies. My two grammar-school siblings garnered little attention from my parents and were rarely held accountable for established family rules. My twin sister and I refused to go to church, retreated into our schoolwork, and focused on heading off to college.

Swerve number one.

My youngest sister's death influenced my college major. Instead of the business coursework my father had insisted upon, I studied psychology. I yearned to understand grief and loss, relationships and personality, and nature versus nurture. My college major set me up with basic knowledge and skills, some of which I would draw on when I launched my adoption probe in 2010.

Swerve number two.

In 2008, when I was forty-eight, married, and raising four busy kids, I flunked a routine mammogram and was sent for a breast biopsy. The need for family medical history became real. To connect with my birth parents, I first had to get my adoption papers from my adoptive parents. This request did not go over well with my adoptive mom. Thanks to my psychology background, I was tuned in on how to frame that difficult conversation, and I was sensitive to Mom's touchpoints. I appealed to her sensibilities as a mother. I explained I desired my birth family's health history, not simply for myself but for my four children.

When the search for my birth relatives heated up in 2011, genetic genealogy was in its early stages. It was not nearly as effective as current DNA testing in helping estranged family members connect. Without my birth parents' true identities and due to the low number of subscribers at that time, DNA testing could not help me solve my adoption riddle. Forced to investigate other search options, I experienced success with the Confidential Intermediary Service of Illinois (CISI). The intermediary located my birth mother, and months later, I received half of my family health history. My benign breast biopsy led to unlocking the longed-for secrets from my closed adoption story.

The big swerve.

As I continued to search for my absent birth father, I picked up an old habit: journaling, and then I enrolled in a creative writing program. Through my coursework, I began to put on paper how I felt about being adopted and what it was like to grow up as a twin and an adoptee, and I outlined my adoption search saga.

A midlife adoption probe rekindled my love of writing. I set up an author platform, launched a blog, and found a publisher for my memoir, *Twice a Daughter*—the tale of my five-year search for personal history. When I finished the final edits of my memoir, our nation was in the early stages of the pandemic. As we all fought to create meaning in our changed world, I realized something important. As a result of writing my memoir, I had grown to accept my closed adoption. I had forgiven it for all it had taken from me, and I was ready to move on to the next chapter in my life.

Somehow a breast biopsy led to finding my birth family, which inspired me to pick up writing, and that hobby morphed into a later-in-life second career. Had I not experienced significant health issues, I may have let my adoption stay where it wanted to be—locked up like a dirty little secret. And if that had happened, I might never have become a writer. Like Michelle Obama, the examination of the pivotal moments in my life has led me to a deeper understanding of my life and pointed me toward a deeper purpose.

Like the former First Lady, I'm grateful for all the swerves.

THE IMPORTANCE OF
"PERSONAL STORY"

It was the fall of 2017, and I was in the hot seat. Several chapters of my memoir were up for critique before a writer's group I had joined through the University of Chicago Writer's Studio. Prior to the session, I'd emailed my classmates a synopsis of my work-in-progress and twelve pages of material from the midpoint of my adoption search to critique. The chapters dealt with the pivotal moment when my birth mother denied my request for contact. While this section of the memoir had been percolating in my head for months, the words were fresh on the printed page. I expected the workshop to expose what worked in the draft, highlight what might be confusing to the reader, and reveal the areas needing revision.

Any writer who has been workshopped knows that presenting one's work is not for the emotionally fragile or vulnerable. To receive critique, writers are warned ahead of time to check their egos at the door. Often during the peer review process, the writer being workshopped scribbles notes while fellow wordsmiths carve up their manuscript. In many workshops, the writer is discouraged from entering the discussion. With many craft classes under my belt, I had thus far survived this kind of creative scrutiny without hiring a therapist (although, after a rigorous critique session, I'm prone to bypass my writing space for several days, replacing my writing time with long, reflective walks).

Once our class settled in, the workshop instructor signaled that I was first on the agenda. I pulled out my stapled chapters and introduced my draft, explaining it was from a work-in-progress—a memoir about the search for my birth relatives. I prepared to read an excerpt.

A young man, about my oldest daughter's age, injected a loud query. "What do you consider your story to be about?"

My head snapped up. The question dumbfounded me. Either my classmate had not read what I'd provided before the class, or I had failed to effectively explain the scope of my work.

Blinking hard in his direction, I found my voice. "This is about my search for 'personal story.'"

Personal story is a catch-all term that adoptees use that incorporates the details of their lives before and after adoption. Until I found my birth relatives, my personal story held only the facts specific to my adoptive family—a German and Irish Catholic couple from the western suburbs of Chicago with infertility issues. In 2014, shortly after I turned fifty-five, my personal story filled in with details that ranged from a family farm in Minnesota to blood that contains Chippewa and Cree Indian and ancestors who were not Catholic but Messianic Jews. It had taken me fifty years to assemble the hodgepodge of facts that explained all of who I was and who I had come to be.

For most folks, "personal story" is a given, a privilege, a right that is presumed or taken for granted. But an adoptee from a closed adoption not only lacks an accurate medical history, the individual is often forbidden by law to know the state where their biological relatives originated or currently reside. For adoptees like me, the possession of basic genealogy or family medical history is a need so profound that until we possess it, it's buried neatly next to other impossible desires like winning the lottery or owning an island.

"What does that mean?" my colleague volleyed back.

I assessed his demeanor and filled my chest with breath.

I'd entered class that night with the intent of discussing my writing. I wanted to go through each page of the draft, hear what word choices were off, where I might have missed a comma, and where I should start a new paragraph. The lingering discussion of "personal story" was sidelining the discussion of my work, but as my lungs filled, I realized for the class to assess my narrative they needed to understand the narrator. Plopping my classmates into part two of my memoir had cheated them out of essential backstory.

I set my pen down and wiped my palms on my khakis. Twelve sets of eyes bored into me as I explained my search for "personal story" meant learning basic information about my biological family and exploring my sense of self. The circumstances of my birth and why I was adopted were the first questions I wanted to solve. Secondly, I desired details regarding my birth parents, such as their physical characteristics, true identities, whereabouts, medical history, and genealogy. So too, I craved family photographs.

I went on to say that in a closed adoption like mine, adoptees are often blocked from information sharing due to a state's privacy laws. While adoption law varies across the country, in many states the rights of the birth and adoptive parents still preclude the adoptee's right to information. In *open adoption* there is an established flow of information and contact between an adoptee, birth parent(s), and the adoptive parent(s). I emphasized the child in an *open adoption* has a better sense of their "personal story" than one from a *closed adoption*.

While my writing group didn't offer much discussion regarding the words that I had printed out for them on the 8½ × 11 stapled sheets, I exited the class meeting with their written critiques to review at home. In turn, I left them with something to consider: the importance of possessing a "personal story" and an introduction to the critical differences between *closed* and *open adoption*.

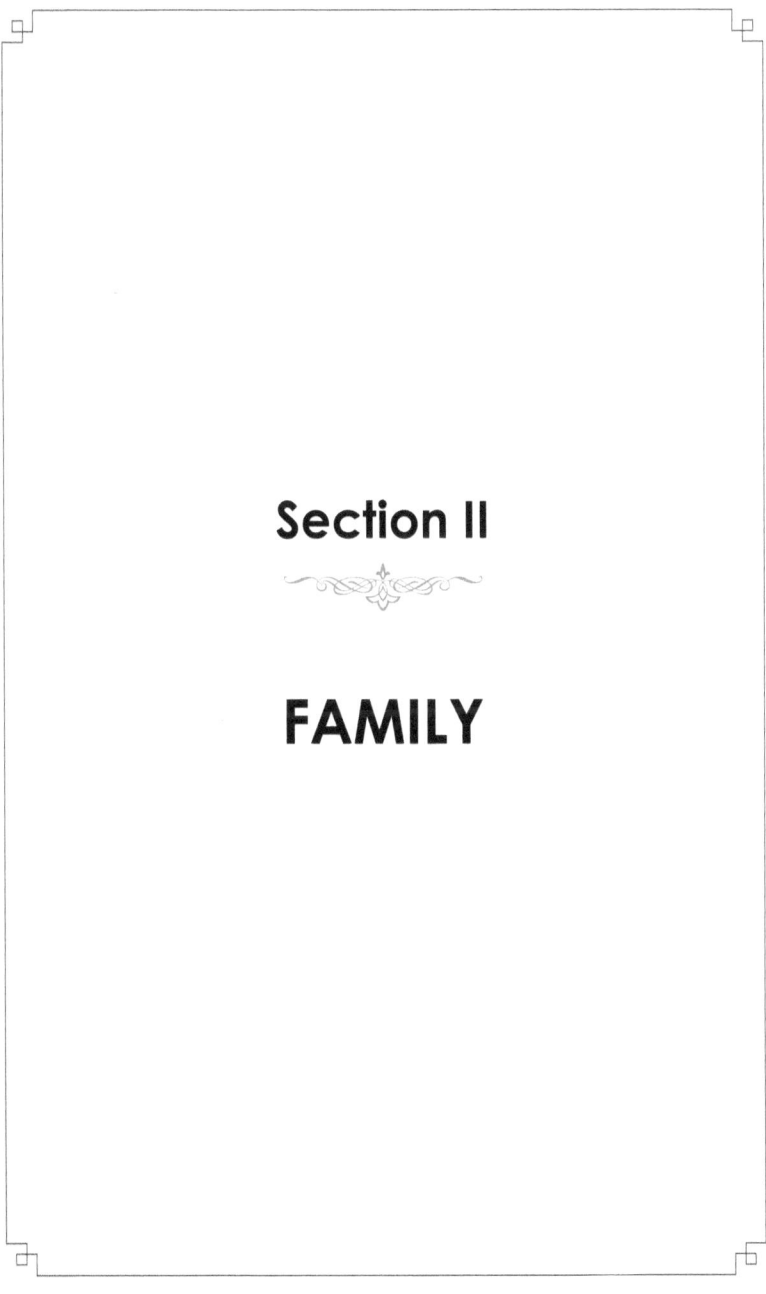

Section II

FAMILY

BIRTH PARENTS HAVE FEARS
AND FANTASIES, TOO

I have written before about the fantasies and fears common among adoptees. In general, we muse about *where do I come from, why was I adopted, who are my biological parents, do I look like either of them, do they think about me,* and *will they come back for me someday.* As adoptees mature, we have anxiety around this notion: since our birth parents already relinquished us, if we don't behave, will our adoptive parents do the same? Many adoptees delay searching for birth relatives due to loyalty to their adoptive parents. Adoptee fantasies also revolve around what life would have been like if adoption hadn't occurred, what a search for birth relatives might disclose, and if a reunion with the family of origin is likely or possible.

Just like adoptees, birth parents have fears and fantasies, too!

When I entered reunion with my birth mother in 2011, I learned firsthand about some of her fears. Because she was born in the 1930s, how she felt about her unwed pregnancy had much to do with the social values and customs of her time. Women married first, *then* they had babies. This is in sharp contrast to today's acceptable practice of bearing a child either *in* or *out* of wedlock.

Even though my birth mother was living on her own and supporting herself when she learned she was pregnant with my twin sister and me, she feared being shunned by her parents and siblings. Her shame was so real that she moved out of state with a girlfriend to avoid discovery. Because of the customs of the day, my birth mother was forced into choosing adoption over parenting. For five decades, she lived with the painful secret of giving birth and relinquishing two daughters.

My birth mom was a third-grade teacher. When my twin sister and I entered reunion with her, she admitted that whenever she saw twin girls, her thoughts went immediately to us. She studied the faces, coloring, and mannerisms of the girls for clues as to whether she was looking at her birth daughters. Like other birth mothers, she pondered where we lived, what had happened to us, and whether we were alive and well. She prayed we were in a good home and healthy and happy. She also wondered if our adoptive parents had kept the names she gave us at birth and if we'd been told about our adoption.

In my first conversation with my birth mother, she wanted to know why I had chosen this point in my life to seek her out. I explained my primary desire was to have a sense of family health history, and I was also curious about our genealogy. My birth mom was surprised to learn some of the information she provided to the adoption agency had not been disseminated to our adoptive parents. Research shows many birth parents wonder what information has been passed on to the child they placed for adoption.

For a birth parent, the overwhelming fear is that their child will not want contact if they reach out. Birth mothers report that placing a child for adoption involves a powerful sense of loss and isolation (A. Brodzinsky, 1990). These feelings are true for closed and open adoptions. Clinicians report that the birth mothers they see in therapy complain about continued shame, depression, trauma, unresolved grief, and a negative self-image. Many women believe because they gave away a child, they are therefore unlovable. Much like adoptees, birth mothers wonder what life would have been like if they had not chosen adoption, what a search might reveal, and if reunion is possible.

WHAT SHOULD YOU CALL
YOUR BIRTH MOTHER?

If you were to enter reunion with your birth mother, would you call her Mom, Mother, her first name, or something else?

Before I began searching for my birth mom, she was just "Mother" to me. I know it sounds distant and impersonal, but it was all I had to work with. She was my womb, a woman who "wasn't," "didn't want to be," or "couldn't be" in my life. *Mother* was a private label, a pet name if you will. I called her this in my thoughts and journals.

I was born in the Baby Scoop Era, that time between World War II and the 1970s when a flood of white babies hit the adoption scene. At that time, almost all adoptions were closed. All the identifying information for my biological parents was sealed under court order. It protected the privacy of all parties involved. As a result, I had no first or last name by which to call my biological mom. "Mother" became ingrained in me for fifty years.

In 2011, the Illinois adoption statutes changed. It became legal to request the information on a sealed original birth record (OBR). The redacted birth certificate I occasionally pulled out to renew my passport held my adoptive parents' names. All evidence of my other parent set had been stricken, hidden in some dusty file cabinet in the basement of the Illinois Department of Vital Records.

During this period, I was three years deep into a search for my birth mom. I had located her through Midwest Adoption's Confidential Intermediary Program. She had denied my first request for contact but later changed her mind. When I received my OBR, I already knew the neat cursive signature on the OBR was an alias. My birth mom had been in my life for over a year. I was no longer calling her "Mother." My sister and I had decided to call her by her first name.

I never considered calling my biological mother Mom. "Mom" was reserved for someone else, the woman that nurtured me into adulthood. Mom was the soother of midnight tears, owned the cure for constipation, and dished out "the talk" when I was eleven. She cheered all my successes and mourned my daily hurts, helped me think through the problems of the day, and set me straight on a moral course. Mom was my adoptive mom/mother and A-mom. She was my "psychological" mother.

Birth mom or *birth mother* was the label I used when talking to others about the mysterious stranger who carried my twin sister and me to full term and left us in the care of Catholic Charities in Chicago in 1959. Often this mother has other titles: *biological mom, bio-mom, B-mom, first mother, other mother,* or *natural mother.*

I would be remiss if I didn't bring up the controversial designation of *real mom*. There is much discussion as to who is the "real" mother: the adoptive mother who raises her adopted child or the biological mother who gave birth to that child. My inclination is to proclaim they are both real because they both play a role in an adoptee's life. In the end, it's personal opinion.

One may feel more real than the other, given the adoption situation.

So, when thinking about what to call the woman from whom you were separated through adoption, I urge all adoptees to consider the matter carefully. Read what the literature advises. Consult other adoptees and advisors like social workers or counselors. See what feels right as it rolls off your tongue. Whatever you decide is the correct name for this special person.

THE OTHER MOTHER'S DAY

Unless you are an adoptee or a birth mom, you're probably unaware that National Birth Mother's Day is celebrated on the Saturday before Mother's Day. Until I launched the search for my birth mom, I had no idea that birth mothers are recognized on a different day than traditional mothers.

When my adoption search hit a major roadblock early in 2011, the social worker facilitating the adoption search and reunion for Catholic Charities invited me to attend a group meeting made up of adoptees, birth parents, and adoptive families. On a Saturday afternoon in early May, I joined twenty or so adults in a conference room at Catholic Charities in downtown Chicago.

The social worker opened our session by acknowledging that Mother's Day was less than a week away. Her bright blue eyes nodded warmly at each of us clustered around the U-shaped conference table.

She stated, "This is a day that brings both joy and heartache, depending on which side of the adoption equation you are on."

Several women at one end grabbed tissues from the boxes at the center of the table. In a few minutes, I would learn that these ladies were birth mothers. Thus far, they had been unsuccessful in entering reunion with the children they placed for adoption.

The social worker continued, "As we go around the table, please state your first name, whether you're an adoptee, birth parent, adoptive parent, or a loved one, and then let us know how you plan to celebrate Mother's Day this year."

One of the teary-eyed birth moms raised her hand.

She said, "I want to remind everyone that Saturday, the day before Mother's Day, is National Birth Mother's Day."

The social worker nodded vigorously at the group. "Thank you. I'm sorry I neglected to mention this in the opening. For those new to the group, Birth Mother's Day was established in 1990 by a group of birth mothers to remember their adopted child, cope with that loss, and educate society about the complexities of the adoption experience. Please go on."

The birth mother then shared with the group about how she hoped to receive a reply to a letter she'd recently written to the birth daughter she placed for adoption thirty years earlier. And then she uttered words that made me hold my breath.

"As delighted as I am to celebrate Mother's Day with my mother and family, the year I can openly observe Birth Mother's Day with the daughter I lost to adoption will be one of the happiest moments of my life. Until that happens though, I will honor Birth Mother's Day in silence."

Our moderator studied the somber faces of our group and asked, "How many of you are part of an open adoption experience?"

Several of the younger people raised their hands.

The social worker continued, "In open adoption, it's not uncommon for adoptive parents to send flowers and cards to the birth mother along with recent photos of their child. Some even call the birth mom as a way of honoring her on Birth Mother's Day."

A man who looked to be in his forties spoke up next. He said, "I send each of my mothers a card for Mother's Day. On Birth Mother's Day I make it a point to phone my birth mom. This is our special day, and we talk about this. On the following day, I do the same for the mom who raised me. Having separate days to celebrate with my mothers is important to me. And to them."

As the group members went around and slowly introduced themselves, some, like me, responded that they had not known about Birth Mother's Day. Other adoptees, lucky enough to be in reunion with their birth moms, stated their birth mothers preferred to be honored on Mother's Day. Given my recently stalled search, I doubted whether I'd get the opportunity to acknowledge my birth mom on Birth Mother's Day or Mother's Day.

That was my first experience of attending a post-adoption support group meeting. Not only was it the moment I first learned about a day dedicated solely to birth moms, but it was also the first time I witnessed a birth mom's heartache. It was a sobering moment, one I will never forget, and I have drawn upon it heavily in trying to understand the actions of my birth mom.

When I finally connected with my birth mother, we established our Mother's Day routine. Because my birth mom lives in another state—and I have my children to celebrate with during Mother's Day weekend—my twin sister and I visit her the first weekend in May. By splitting our celebrations, we give our birth mom the attention she deserves and honor our adoptive mom on her special day.

Over a decade ago, I hadn't known about the other Mother's Day, and I certainly had my doubts about whether it was an event I'd be privileged to experience. This year, besides celebrating the roles that both of my mothers continue to play in my life, I'm grateful that both survived the COVID-19 pandemic.

BIRTH MOMS SHOULD COME
WITH WARNING LABELS

What *I wish I'd known* sums up the years it took to locate and connect with my birth mother.

Before I decided to launch the search for her, I researched the idea. I borrowed, perused, and ordered a collection of books, all dealing with adoption and adoption search and reunion. My copies of Ann Fessler's *The Girls That Went Away* and Betty Jean Lifton's *Lost & Found* are so dog-eared and marked up that I refuse to lend them out. The time I spent reading and processing information was not just about how to go about locating birth relatives. It was also about evaluating the costs of each search alternative, the expected timeframes, and the likely pitfalls I'd probably experience.

Besides collecting the stack of self-help books, I sought advice. The social worker assigned to my case through the confidential intermediary program at Midwest Adoption Center in Des Plaines, Illinois, became a trusted friend. In addition, I became a regular at the quarterly post-adoption support group meetings offered through Catholic Charities. These marathon roundtables were comprised of adult adoptees, birth parents, adoptive parents, and significant others. This constellation of people touched by adoption was ably moderated by a licensed social worker.

In these group meetings, we listened to one another and shared our vulnerabilities: what it's like to give up/place a child for adoption; what it feels like to be adopted; what it is like to parent an adopted child; the pitfalls and peaks of searching; and the successes and failures of reunion. These hours-long events left me drained and depleted, but I gathered the knowledge I needed.

Even with all the prep work these meetings provided, I still wasn't ready for what was to come. I missed valuable cues offered by the birth mothers in my peer support group. And, in my reading, I neglected or glossed over vital warnings: Reunion is rarely, if ever, a quick, straight path to a blissful outcome. Managing one's expectations is vital. No amount of reading or therapy can prepare an adoptee, birth parent, or adoptive parent for the rigors of adoption search and reunion. There is no typical search, no prescribed reunion, and no right or wrong way to find the folks you want to include in your life. Your route is yours. You must craft it as you go.

Often, I stumbled along the path to locate my birth family. I wish I'd been warned about the intense anger a birth mom might express when found. When that unbounded, fear-laced anger was directed at me, I felt sucker punched. I'd been harboring a fantasy about being the lost girl found, but my birth mom lived in fear that her secret would come out. When my birth mother placed my twin sister and me for adoption, she'd been told her privacy would be protected. In her view, my contact violated this agreement. Neither the intermediary nor I could have known she'd react in such a vehement manner.

Once my birth mom came around and welcomed me into her life, we had other issues to address. It became apparent that protecting my birth mother's reputation was a higher priority to her than developing a healthy relationship with me. On one visit to her hometown, we were seated in a public restaurant, and she chose not to acknowledge me as her daughter. Instead, she introduced me to the waitress as a "friend visiting from Chicago."

I was crushed. Intellectually, I knew she was transferring her shame about being an unwed mother onto me, but her attitude was nonetheless hurtful. She was embarrassed to be seen with me. After a sustained cooling-off period and many painful conversations about boundaries, our reunion got back on track—we now talk regularly and share what's happening in our lives. But this incident and others highlighted that my birth mom's shame had led to a life where keeping secrets and harboring half-truths was acceptable.

Her ease in providing mistruths and misconceptions was unsettling and continued during the early years of our reunion. She derailed my search for my birth father by incorrectly spelling his name. Once I located him through another source, she admitted she had lied out of fear.

Before my search I would not have believed that anger, shame, lies, rejection, disrespect, and a repeated lack of acknowledgment would color my adoption search and reunion. Sadly, they did, and I had to turn to social workers for advice on how to move past these obstructions. All told, it took more than five years to complete my adoption searches and get the reunion with my birth mom in a comfortable place.

Adoption is complicated. I knew that before starting my search. While the readings and research prepared me for the twisted course of my probe, they did not adequately portray the intensity of potential outcomes. I now realize the woman who brought me into this world, the life she led, and the social mores of the 1950s deeply affected her unpredictable behavior. But I wish I had known more about her and been given a list of warnings before blundering into contact in a system that set us up as adversaries. Perhaps we all wish we could see into the future to be better prepared for the road ahead.

SECONDARY REJECTION

Secondary *rejection* is a well-known term in the adoption world. It refers to the disappointment, hurt, or rejection that adoptees and/or birth relatives experience as they attempt to connect with the family members they lost to adoption. The first rejection is adoption itself, which Nancy Verrier aptly termed the "primal wound."

Secondary rejection appears in many forms:

- a birth mother's reluctance to share the secret of her unwed pregnancy with a spouse or family member.

- a refusal by either a birth parent or an adoptee to facilitate introductions to relatives and friends.

- a refusal to share health history and background information.

- an unwillingness to inform or to include a relative in daily activities, holidays, or special events.

Secondary rejection is also a phone call that takes too long to be returned or a letter that goes unanswered for months. Each time one of these snubs, denials, or dismissals occurs, it reminds us of our lack of importance in another's life. Each of these slights, big or small, is yet another wound to a heart already compromised because of adoption.

When I first reached out to my birth mom through an intermediary in 2011, I experienced the first of many secondary rejections. It came as a note to the intermediary denying any and all requests for contact and warning me to never reach out to my birth mom again. It took me months to peel myself off the ground. As a mom, I couldn't understand how a mother could treat her child in this unloving, disrespectful manner.

To deal with this shocking and unexpected assault on my ego and identity, I joined a post-adoption support group. Comprised of my peers, this group supported me as I learned the appropriate skills to utilize in coping with secondary rejection. Over many meetings, I understood and had empathy for the unique circumstances that led to my birth mother's secondary rejection—her denial of contact.

Eventually, my birth mom had a change of heart, and I was eager to connect with her. Yet, months into our full-blown reunion, there were small setbacks. My phone calls sometimes went unreturned. My birth mom was unwilling to widen the circle of "who knows." The first time my twin sister and I visited the senior living complex where our birth mom and stepdad had moved, she refused to let us sign in at the front desk.

Over lunch that day, she confessed that she hadn't wanted us to write in the guestbook because next to our names was a space for "relationship to resident." Apparently, no one at the senior center had been informed that she had two biological daughters. She explained the facility was like living in a fishbowl, and she didn't want the shameful scrutiny of her peers. I bristled. If we hadn't been sitting in a crowded restaurant, I might have argued with her about the hurtfulness of her actions. I felt minimized. Later, the situation worsened as we strolled the senior center hallway back to her unit. To whomever we came across, my twin sister and I were introduced as "relatives visiting from Chicago."

When I returned home, I first called my peer support group members. I was reminded to treat myself with kindness and to surround myself with people who treated me lovingly. And once I was ready to establish a positive connection with my birth mom, I would need to set boundaries.

And so, with great trepidation that my pushback would anger my birth mom and put our newly formed ties in jeopardy, I expressed how her recent behavior had made me feel: unworthy and less-than. My words were received with coolness. Our reunion hit a speed bump, and months passed before we chatted by phone again. We worked it out and are now ten years into our reunion.

Several weeks ago, my stepdad had a slip-and-fall in the bathroom. It resulted in a head wound, a broken neck, and several broken bones. I found out about the mishap not from my birth mom but by email from a first cousin with whom I've become friendly. I stewed about why my birth mom had neglected to inform me firsthand and in a timely manner. I checked in with her, and because of her distraught state, I decided not to confront her about leaving me off the list of "who knows." A week later, I got another email from the same cousin expressing her condolences over my stepdad's sudden death.

My heart sank on two counts.

First, I mourned my stepdad—a man whose kindness and easy acceptance of me when I entered his world ten years ago— had met no parallel. Then, I grieved over the secondary rejection from my birth mom: my sister and I had been deliberately left off the chain of information.

When I opened the email about my stepdad's death, I was out to dinner with my son and his fiancé. We'd spent the day finalizing their wedding plans. As I shared my shocking news, my son enveloped me in a hug.

"I'm sorry, Mom," he said. "About your stepdad. And about how you heard about it."

When my future daughter-in-law drew me into her arms and hugged me tightly, I realized I was right where I needed to be. I was among family who cared about me, loved ones who treated me with dignity and respect and who acknowledged that the rejection tearing up my insides was valid.

The next morning, I called my birth mom. After I expressed my sadness and sympathies, she explained my presence at the funeral would complicate her life. Because my stepdad's relatives were scattered over a three-state area, she had never seen the merit in informing them about the twin daughters she had placed for adoption and who had recently returned to her life.

When I got off the phone with my eighty-eight-year-old mother, a woman once an unwed mother and who grieved a different kind of loss, I sighed. And I sighed again. After a decade of receiving countless secondary rejections, I wasn't angry anymore. I wasn't feeling hurt or rejected either. I felt sorry for her, and I grieved for her.

The pain and shame of being an unwed mother in the 1950s and safeguarding that secret for a lifetime had formed my mother's personality and behavior. As much as I wish it could all be different, I understood. It was easier for my mother to keep my twin sister and me out of the funeral events so she could preserve her dignity.

A modern birth mom who experienced more transparency in her adoption plan might have elected to surround herself with her only daughters so that they could participate in the grieving process. Sadly, my mother is from an older generation, and her habits and attitudes are entrenched and not easily discarded.

While secondary rejection is tough to receive, it is not about hurting others intentionally. The attitudes and behaviors that produce secondary rejection come from fear and self-preservation. They are about controlling and managing the stressors inherent in the adoption experience. However unwarranted, unexpected, or unjust, some secondary rejection is inevitable.

As adoptees and birth parents entering reunion with the family we lost through adoption, we must realize we can control only one aspect of secondary rejection: our reaction to it.

In response to secondary rejection, we can choose to set boundaries for what we can or will not tolerate; we can select from a vast array of professional support; we can choose to withdraw from any relationship or setting that endangers our sense of self; and we can surround ourselves with people who treat us with the love and respect that we both crave and deserve.

TWO TOUGH CONVERSATIONS
WITH MY ADOPTIVE MOTHER

Before I was old enough to know what it meant, I learned my twin sister and I were adopted. Usually around our birthday, my adoptive parents would call my sister and me into the living room to discuss our adoption. During these talks I learned that my folks waited six long years to become parents; how badly they had "wanted" my twin sister and me; and that they would assist us should we desire to research our adoption. I heard their words, but an inner sense told me that my adoption story was "better left alone"; digging into it might upset my parents. Because I felt loved and that my place in my family was secure, deferring an adoption probe was an easy decision.

My perspective about "leaving well enough alone" changed when I began to have health issues as I neared middle age. The first obstacle was that I could not start such a quest without first speaking to my adoptive parents. My adoption papers were in their safe deposit box. For whatever reason, they had never passed them on to my sister or me.

Tough conversation #1:

I knew my audience, so it was an easy prediction: my adoptive father would support my efforts, but my adoptive mom would be disappointed and upset. I suspected Mom would feel threatened by our birth mother reentering our lives. So, I decided the tricky conversation should occur in stages. This would allow everyone time to adjust to what was in the offing.

Step 1: I explained that due to some health issues, I wanted my birth family's medical history. I needed my adoption papers to get started. Mom said she'd speak to my dad about locating the documents. I'd dropped two bombs: my health was in jeopardy, and I wanted to launch an adoption search. The conversation was short. I counted on my mother's concern for my health to ease the shock of looking for my family of origin.

Step 2: I set a date to meet with them and collect the paperwork. I prepared my comments with great care: I loved them; my search was not about how I felt about them or the job they had done as parents; their role as my parents was secure; and I'd enlighten them at every stage. As predicted, Dad quickly said he understood while my mom did not hide her displeasure.

The Outcome: The search for my birth relatives had many starts and stops, and I was forced to change search angels several times. Here's a recap of the issues: my birth mom used an alias on my OBR; the Illinois adoption law changed in 2011; my birth mom was initially reluctant to connect; and she gave me an incorrect spelling of my birth dad's last name. Over the years that I spent digging into my personal story, I tried to update my adoptive parents. Through the ups and downs, I had the sense Mom was relieved when my birth relatives seemed destined to be strangers.

Tough conversation #2:

There was a six-month period during which my birth mom first denied my request for contact, then abruptly changed her mind. Our reunion was swift. In two months, we progressed from exchanging letters through an intermediary to regular phone calls and then a face-to-face meeting. During these months, my adoptive father was in poor health. I had to decide when to disclose these developments to my adoptive parents: immediately (knowing it might add to the stress they were already under) or later (after my adoptive dad had recuperated).

Step 1: I decided to wait to disclose my contact with my birth mom until my adoptive dad recuperated. This meant that my parents would learn about the meeting with my birth mom after it happened. While I felt that delaying my news was the prudent option, it also felt dishonest. Sometimes what feels wrong is right.

Step 2: I scheduled a time to meet with my folks at their apartment. I rehearsed the sequence of shocking news: my birth mom had changed her mind about connecting, we'd exchanged letters and phone calls, and we met in person.

The Outcome: I hoped my adoptive mother would be relieved I'd finally claimed my family background and health history. I also hoped after all the heartache and years of obstacles, my adoptive mother might be pleased for me. Within minutes of learning that I had met my birth mom, my adoptive mother stated she did not want "that woman" in her life.

My dad and I were stunned. When my mother assumed this stance, I chose not to share any reunion news or updates regarding searches for other birth relatives. Four years skipped by, and thankfully my mom softened. She shocked me by agreeing to exchange letters with my birth mom. My father remained supportive. I believe he was instrumental in lifting my mother through her doubts.

In summary, I have two comments about these scenarios. First, like many adoptees I chose to wait until later in life to begin my adoption search because I feared ruining my relationship with my adoptive parents. Second, despite the numerous difficulties I faced in owning my personal story, I would tackle this again. Having a complete picture of my existence is a treasure I didn't know I craved and didn't think was possible. Nor did I anticipate how complete I would feel because of it.

THE ONLY THING
MY FATHER GAVE ME

As I filled out my online application to an elite, year-long memoir course, my absent father wasn't even a whisper in my subconscious. I entered the book concept and the working title, attached my latest author bio, and then uploaded the first ten pages of my new manuscript. Having done all the hard steps first, I focused on the form's remaining queries.

"Enter your birthdate, *optional."

Thoughts swirled in my head. By asking this, was the selection committee looking for older authors with a lifetime of experiences to reveal, seasoned voices with oodles to reflect upon? Or was the program leaning toward selecting younger authors to nurture, writers with edgier tones who might express themselves in more experimental structures? Then again, perhaps the question meant the program had a bent toward a cross-section of students, thereby representing writers of all ages, voices, and writing styles.

I stared at the optional birthdate box.

If I entered not just the month and day of my birth, but the actual year in which I was born, was I less likely to be chosen? *What the heck*, I reasoned. I am what I am: a middle-aged woman, a mother, and a grandma; a lifelong journaler who found her birth relatives and realized she suddenly had a story to tell (one that someone might need to hear); and a relative newbie to this online writing submission process.

I sighed and tapped out the whole darn thing, birth year and all.

Okay, next question: "Enter your race/ethnicity."

For most of my life, this has been an easy question to answer. Adopted at three weeks old with my twin sister, our adoptive parents were told that we'd come from German and Irish ancestry. Our adoption was closed, which meant adoption statutes prevented us from knowing anything about our birth circumstances or birth family. For half a century, I have identified with my adoptive parents' heritage: German, Irish, and Bohemian.

All that changed in 2010.

After years of searching, my twin sister and I reunited with our birth mother. We learned that besides French and German, Cree Indian trickles through our maternal bloodline. Four years later, I located our birth father, and our genealogy expanded to include Scotland, Ireland, and another Native American tribe. One-quarter Chippewa, my birth dad grew up near a reservation in northern Minnesota. For the first fifty-five years of my life, I had no choice but to claim "white" as my ethnicity. Genetics has proven that I can claim Native American, too.

I contemplated the ethnicity box. Breath built in my chest. My hands twisted in my lap.

Since I had been honest about my age, I determined that for the first time in my life, I could and wanted to claim my rightful heritage. In the answer box where my cursor sat blinking, I typed *White and Native American*. Then I sat back in my desk chair and smiled at the screen. The grin was not because I had chosen to be brazenly honest, nor was it pleasure over the newness of selecting *Native American* as my ethnicity on a silly form. It was something else entirely.

When I located my birth father in 2014, I sent him a letter asking for his family medical history. He complied by mail with this caveat: *I may or may not be your biological father. Here's the information you requested. Do not contact me again.* Despite the efforts of my new half-siblings, my birth dad refused to acknowledge my twin and me as his offspring.

In 2017, the man who passed on his Native American ancestry to me died suddenly of a heart attack. We never met in person, nor did we communicate after that first exchange of letters. The sum total of all that my birth father passed on to me amounts to this: a completed health history form, my half-brother's positive DNA match, and the subsequent knowledge that I am Native American.

So, my smile over having filled in the ethnicity box on the course application was about knowing and claiming. Knowing who I am and where I came from and claiming my true heritage.

I suspected my chances of gaining admission into the elite memoir-writing program were slim. Yet, until the adoption search, I knew nothing about my birth relatives, family health history, or genealogy. For decades, I never expected to own any of that. Life is about taking chances, assimilating rejection, and getting back out there. Writing encompasses those same things.

Sitting back in my desk chair, I grinned and pressed submit, and then I silently thanked my birth dad. I hoped if my age was a negative in the eyes of the admission committee, my writing skill and heritage would more than make up for it.

ADOPTIVE PARENTS: DON'T MAKE YOUR CHILD'S ADOPTION SEARCH AN EITHER-OR PROPOSITION

Ultimatums are tough. In business and life, stipulations and requirements can be deal breakers. They can also terminate or damage relationships.

If you are an adoptee and your adoptive parent(s) does not support your desire to investigate your adoption nor do they welcome your reunion with birth relatives, then you are in a tough spot. An adoptee who pushes through or ignores an adoptive parent's objections to achieve those goals will undoubtedly land in an emotional minefield.

A fellow adoptee I know was thrust into such a decision nightmare. The younger of two children, Tom is the only adoptee in his family. He is in his mid-thirties, married, and a father of two adorable girls. His wife, a woman he's known since college, encourages and supports his quest to connect with his birth family. For the last few years, Tom has tackled the numerous barriers intrinsic to unlocking a closed adoption.

When Tom located his birth parents through an intermediary, he learned that they'd been a pair of single college kids when he was placed for adoption. After college, Tom's birth parents married and had another boy and two girls. Tom has three full biological siblings. Stung by the news that he was the only child placed for adoption, he yearned to meet his birth family. An intermediary informed him that they were ready to enter reunion, too.

Here's the glitch: Throughout searching for his birth family, Tom had not shared his journey with his adoptive family.

When he was ready, Tom and his wife gathered his adoptive family around and laid it out: his search, married birth parents, three full siblings, and desire to connect with them. When queried if they'd like to meet his birth family, Tom's parents did not just say no; they made a proclamation. If he persisted in reuniting with the "other" family, he would be dead to them. Tom's adoptive parents insisted he choose: them or us. This ultimatum shoved Tom into a horrible quandary.

The disclosure of my adoption search to my adoptive folks had a slightly different outcome than Tom's. In theory, my parents were supportive. Periodically, I offered updates about the ongoing searches, the first one for my birth mother, then a later one for my birth dad. While my adoptive parents did not issue any ultimatums, they did not offer me any assistance beyond handing over my adoption papers.

When my birth mom denied my request for contact, my adoptive mother said, "That's unfortunate. I was looking forward to meeting her." At the time, I appreciated her show of support. It felt genuine.

Six months later, my birth mom changed her mind. Our contact began with letters, then moved quickly to phone calls, and within six weeks we were in a face-to-face reunion. It was glorious. Shortly after meeting my birth mom, I sat down with my adoptive folks to share the good news, just like Tom had done.

My mouth fell open when Mom said, "I do not want that woman in my life."

Those words seared me. Still do.

Like my fellow adoptee Tom, I was thrust into a delicate situation. Although I fared better than Tom, I was stricken by the unfairness of my predicament. I could maintain contact with my birth mother, but my adoptive mom wanted nothing to do with her: no letters, no meetings, no phone calls. To my adoptive mother, it was as if my other parent set had never existed.

Tom must choose between his adoptive and biological parents. I was forced to choose silence. I'm allowed to have a relationship with my birth mother, but I'm not encouraged to discuss it. Regrettably, Tom has not spoken to his adoptive folks in months. He is crushed that he cannot welcome both sets of parents into his life or his daughters' lives.

Like Tom, when I launched my adoption search, I believed I could balance relationships with both of my families. I wanted my adoptive parents to receive my news like mature adults. Tom and I are both disappointed that our respective adoptive parents put us in an either-or situation where everyone loses and nobody gains.

Here's the thing. When an adoptee seeks information about birth relatives, it is for various valid reasons: health, sense of self/ identity, or an innate need for familial history and connection.

Why should an adoptee's yearning "to know" put the adoptee at odds with family?

WILL MY CHILD HATE ME?

When my parents adopted my twin sister and me, no information regarding our birth parents' genealogy or medical history was shared with them. By contrast, open adoption allows for a free flow of information between the adopted child, his/her adoptive parents, and the birth parents. The quality and frequency of that communication vary. Literature suggests the more information a child has about their background, the more well-adjusted they will be as they mature.

Regardless of whether an adoption was closed or open, there is a common thread among adoptees. Even if we were given the reasons for our adoption, every adoptee wonders, "Why did I have to be adopted? Why me?"

In an open adoption, often there is a letter from the birth parent detailing the reasons for the decision. Those of us from the closed adoption era wonder about or make up our reality regarding our biological families. About one-third of the states in our country allow adult adoptees access to their original birth records, while the rest do not. Even if adoptees possess basic facts about their background, we often quiz ourselves, "Why couldn't things have been different?"

Blaming someone else for a difficult situation is part of human nature. As an adoptee, I often thought about my adoption. At times, I struggled with self-worth, identity, and belonging. These feelings hit me hard when I was a teenager and again when I began the search for my birth mother. My feelings about being adopted and my birth parents are complicated, but I never hated them.

Both of my birth parents rejected me when I first reached out to them as a middle-aged woman experiencing health issues. The contact they denied me and the refusal to acknowledge me as a person angered me. Whenever I thought of them and their dismissiveness, I wanted to explode, but I did not hate them.

I wasn't easy to be around during these rejections. I was confused about my birth parents' choices and was disappointed in a system that set my right to information in the crosshairs with my parents' right to privacy. I worked through my anger and confusion with post-adoption counseling. Over time, I accepted my situation, and I grew to understand my birth parents' perspective.

This is a long answer to a simple but compelling question: Will my child hate me?

To birth parents, I would offer this: Yes, the child you place for adoption might hate you for a time, but hopefully they will not hate you always and forever. Adoption is a tough decision. While adoption is a positive experience for many adoptees, for others it is more complicated.

If you are a birth parent contemplating adoption for your unborn child, this fear of what your child will think of you may or may not influence your decision.

Write your child a letter. Explain your situation and thoughts surrounding your decision. Share with your unborn child details about who you are, what you think, and how you feel as a prospective parent. It's easier to dislike a stranger than to hate someone you feel like you know. Consider adding counseling or support groups to your routine to stem the emotions you will face as time goes on.

Having realistic expectations, effective communication, and seeking counseling or support are all part of the solution in dealing with the concern of *will my adopted child hate me?*

WHEN I ADOPTED THEM

I have a confession to make. I was a holdout. My twin sister and I knew at an early age that we were adopted, but we generally avoided thinking or talking about it. It wasn't until I chased down my adoption story—filtered it through the lens that comes with being middle-aged and a parent—that several thoughts crystalized for me.

Until I began researching my adoption, my status as an adoptee had been a detail that I kept private. Beyond extended family, discussing my adoption with others was uncomfortable for me. I needed to know someone well and trust them before revealing personal information like my birth history.

Adoptees like me from the '60s and '70s were usually the products of closed adoptions. We knew little if anything about our background. We had not been given any health history or genealogy, and we were prohibited from communicating with our family of origin. Most of us didn't know the circumstances that led to our being placed in a closed adoption.

While I kept my adoption hidden from others, I inwardly suppressed the implications as well. As a young girl, I couldn't dwell on why some woman would not want to parent two perfect little girls. Had we done something wrong, or was it that two were too many? As a teenager—when boys and sex were frequent thoughts—I speculated that my adoption was a result of teen pregnancy. Until I learned the truth mid-way through life, that made-up story satisfied me; it silenced the internal bantering and wondering.

Besides holding back from friends and family and believing a made-up story, I did not fully embrace the idea that my adoptive parents were legitimately mine. A part of me was waiting for my birth parents to return and take me back to where I truly belonged. And when they showed up, I imagined they would be everything I wanted them to be. These loosely held beliefs meant that for most of my life I had not been in an honest relationship with myself or my adoptive parents. Sadly, because I couldn't let go of my "first" parents, I wasn't ever "all in" with Mom and Dad.

If you asked my adoptive mother what I was like as a child, she'd say I was a reserved, serious, and contemplative child. I was prone to taking off in search of a quiet spot in the three-bedroom, two-bath home I shared with my five siblings and parents. I was forever on my bicycle renewing library books or hanging out at the park across the street from our chaotic household. I craved independence and privacy; I relished being alone with my thoughts or creating spaces where I could control my actions and their consequences.

As a young girl, most places that I went, my twin went too. I was never searching for a best friend because I was born with mine. My twindom was an advantage in life, one that I still count as the biggest blessing from my closed adoption. My adoptive mother was always on the outside of our duo. And because I held out for my birth mother to reenter my life, my heart treated my mom as a temp or a stand-in. While this sounds unfair, it's an honesty I came to acknowledge later in life.

Yet, somewhere along the bumpy road of searching for my birth relatives, something astounding happened: I had accepted my adoptive parents as my "real" parents. In a sense, I had adopted them. Perhaps this transformation occurred during my birth mom's denial of contact. Maybe it happened while I waited for the judge to order on my behalf that I deserved my first family's health history. I suspect that when I discovered my birth mother's lies and when my birth father refused to acknowledge me is when I had officially made the leap. Regardless of when this shift transpired, I came to see my adoptive parents for who they were: two honest, decent people who had loved and nurtured me into adulthood.

Now as a middle-aged woman, I readily admit that my "real" parents are the ones that cared for me my entire life. I am grateful to my adoptive parents for the many opportunities they created for me, the love they freely shared, and the sense of family and belonging they imparted. I feel fortunate that they played such an integral role in my life. They are mine, and I belong to them.

It isn't my fault that I was an adoption holdout. The closed adoption system baked that into the cake. One of the many results of my adoption search is that I have reflected upon my relationships and where I fit in with my families and community. I'm relieved the subject of my adoption is no longer off-limits within myself and with others. Most importantly, I accept my birth mother's role in giving me life and revere my adoptive parents for giving me *a* life.

I KNOW IT'S NOT MOTHER'S DAY

May has come and gone and so has the day for publicly honoring mothers and maternal figures. Yet, I would argue we never tire of saluting the women who impact our lives. I know it's not Mother's Day, but I have an overdue tribute to offer.

On September 5, 2014, my diminutive mother-in-law (she shrank from 5' 2" to 4' 10" over her adult life) passed away at eighty-eight. She wasn't just the wise mother of my husband, or simply the doting grandmother to my four children. Mary Lou, "ML," was my trusted confidante, able adviser, and bold co-conspirator. She was also instrumental in my becoming a writer and telling my adoption search story.

For most of the years I knew ML, she flaunted a closely cropped haircut like Audrey Hepburn. Even into her eighties, one had to hover above her to spy the random threads of gray in her nut-brown hair. ML honed her sharp wit and intellect with NPR, The *New Yorker,* and several daily crossword puzzles. In her prime, when most mothers did not work, she edited a publication called *The Sunday Visitor.* Her love of words included stints as a librarian, an adjunct professor teaching senior citizens reminiscence writing, and two demanding book clubs. Wherever she sat in her cozy townhouse, a stack of hardcover library books resided, as well as cigarettes and a full ashtray.

When my children were little, she toted picture books from her local library to read until the kids napped on her lap. Sometimes they accompanied her to the library for a Saturday afternoon children's program or remained strapped in their car seats while ML delivered large-print books to housebound elderly. Getting down on the floor to build Legos or dress dollies was not in her repertoire. Known as "Lil G" by her four grandkids, she was not so much about toys and play but rather about thinking and doing, as in letters, words, writing projects, and Scrabble. ML was a grandmother best suited for big kids, teenagers, and young adults.

I have two other mothers: One who raised me, and the other who passed on her DNA to my twin sister and me. My adoptive mother and I share the familiarity that comes with years of shared experience. Our bond is complicated. When I was three weeks old, Mom got a call from a social worker at Catholic Charities: fraternal twin girls awaited at St. Vincent's Orphanage in downtown Chicago. She was fond of saying that my sister and I are "her gift from God," but we are also a gift from another mother—a woman whom Mom didn't want me to find.

Besides a shared German heritage, my birth mother had something else in common with my adoptive mom. She did not welcome me searching her out. An unwed mother during the late 1950s, an era rife with unforgiving social mores and customs, my birth mother spent years coping with shame and blame. Her pregnancy and our adoption were closely held secrets until I suddenly banged on her door.

During the many years it took to locate my family of origin and assemble a full family health history and genealogy, my project did not interest my adoptive mother. I drew my support from a rooting section comprised of my husband, four children, twin sister, and various friends. And one of the biggest cheerleaders in my family was ML, my mother-in-law.

Here's the thing. Mary Lou wasn't just idly interested in the juicy details of my adoption search. She was *in it*. If she wasn't physically nearby, she was waiting by the phone with her books and cigarettes. As soon as I received my original birth record (OBR), I dialed her number. When the name my birth mother used on the OBR turned out to be an alias, I sought ML's counsel. Her infamous raspy chortle, "Oh, no. You've got to be kidding?" led to a welcome barrage of questions and devising several plan Bs.

As I struggled to own my adoption story while dealing with recurring health concerns, I repeatedly turned to my mother-in-law. I shared countless tales of he-said-she-said-and-this-happened-and-that. All the while, I never once sensed that ML was just letting me talk or that she'd rather have been somewhere else.

ML listened. She heard me. Through the phone lines I could feel her noodling the nuances and ramifications of my adoption probe as if it was one of her grand crossword puzzles.

She'd offer, "Have you thought about . . .?"

Always, before she hung up, I'd hear, "You know you have to write about this. It's too good of a story."

I took her advice.

As a mother and grandmother, ML was adept at encouraging younger generations to expand their minds. As a mother-in-law, you would think she might've taken a step back and not been so forceful in her opinions and ideas, but I'm grateful that this was not her nature. ML made several things clear: she was rooting for me to succeed in locating and developing a relationship with my birth mother; it was vital for me to accept and forgive my adoptive mom's stance on that quest; and I should attempt to heal the widening rift between Mom and me.

Mary Lou McGue, my mother-in-law, died in her home on her terms at eighty-eight. Her death occurred eight months after I shared my first birthday with my birth mother and eighteen months before I located my birth father and two half-siblings. While she did not travel with me across the finish line of my adoption search, I felt her presence and support. I am comforted that she was with me through the toughest times—when I needed her most. From her home study, I inherited personally annotated books on writing and memoir. They have become some of my most prized belongings.

So here I am. Years after my mother-in-law died, I continue to compose my weekly blog and pen a monthly column for my local paper—all things she encouraged me to tackle. My memoir about the search for my birth relatives has been recognized with several book awards. I believe that, from whatever reality her soul is now, ML is cheering for me to press on. She has skin in that game. Kisses, ML; you are not forgotten.

FIRST COUSINS

Cousins are in town for a visit. Not my first cousins, but my husband's. People I have known for nearly four decades. As the years have tumbled into one another, these folks, my husband's next of kin, have become my relatives, too. Not because of my spouse but because of my need to belong to his extended family.

For the past few days, I've busied our relatives with unique local activities and venues. We have drunk far too much alcohol on days normally spent sipping tea and watching Netflix. I have marveled and giggled at family anecdotes, myths, and legends. Between our activities and the sharing of family memories, I muse. I wonder what it would've been like to grow up knowing my blood relations, my first cousins, from my early years onward.

My twin sister and I grew up as the oldest of six. The top half of our family's birth order are adoptees. Since my adoptive mother is the youngest of thirteen, I grew up knowing plenty of first cousins, but they are not my blood relatives. They are my mother's relations, and their numbers continue to climb. It's difficult to develop meaningful bonds with that many first cousins, especially if you meet only once a year at the required family reunion, or at a few weddings and funerals.

My adoptive father had two older sisters, so gathering with his side of the family for holidays was simpler, easier. During my formative years, I developed a bond with a handful of those cousins. We rubbed elbows over turkey and dressing, chased down plastic eggs stuffed with candy in my aunt's yard, and ran rampant after dark playing hide-and-seek or ding-dong-ditch.

Am I satisfied with the smattering of first cousins that color my childhood memories? Yes. Absolutely.

Just as emphatically, I never dreamed I would someday meet any biological first cousins. When I first began my search for family background, I set my sights on gathering their health history and genealogy. That goal morphed into a desire for face-to-face reunions and long-term relationships. I'm proud that contact with my birth mother is entering its second decade. Because my biological mother's unwed pregnancy and her subsequent relinquishment of my twin sister and me was a closely held secret for decades, she was reluctant to widen the circle beyond a handful of people. Months passed before my birth mother introduced me to her closest sister. Several more months elapsed before a second aunt and uncle welcomed me into the family.

Knowing the names and locations of the remaining aunts and uncles was easy, thanks to various genealogical sites. Honoring my birth mother's desire to take things slowly kept me from contacting birth relatives I matched with online. Her privacy and my relationship with her were more important to me than expanding family exponentially. In recent years, my birth mother's secret leaked out. Her living siblings and spouses were shocked to learn their eldest sister had twin daughters approaching sixty, and most were thrilled that we had reentered her life.

When I receive 23andMe notifications that I have new relatives, I am nonplussed. With more and more folks signing up for DNA testing, these emails come regularly, but I almost always click the link to ascertain how closely we match. I never dreamed

I'd see a match with three first cousins. It thrilled me to glimpse names I recognized from the genealogy documents my birth mother had passed on to me. The first cousin connection was a milestone. Still, I debated about whether to reach out or not. Since my birth mother's secret was out, wasn't I free to connect with my relatives now?

Within weeks, two sharply dressed women met my twin sister and me on a clear sunny morning for breakfast at a Chicago restaurant. All of us had traveled some distance to make the gathering happen. What was it like meeting a first cousin? The eagerness the four of us felt as we slid across the leather booth and scooted our chairs in close was apparent. Grins and coffee all around. Similarities were evident: noses, eyes, a gesture here, and a smile there. It was glorious. One for the record books.

Much as my husband and I had done with his cousins recently, the four of us shared stories and laughter. We promised to keep in touch, plan another rendezvous, and let our mothers in on the momentous event. The waitress obliged us with several great cell phone pics, one of which sits in a frame on my desktop. I'm staring at it now. My first set of biological first cousins. Pinch me.

Of course, I consider my other cousins, the ones I grew up with, as mine. Because they are mine. We are legally bound. Adding these two new women, my biological first cousins, to my growing family is a blessing I will continue to praise. And I'm grateful to genetic genealogy for unlocking the chains of my closed adoption.

I don't curse you anymore, closed adoption. I'm glad you finally stepped aside and allowed me to know from whom and where I came from, and to whom I belong.

WHY DO WE DREAM
OF THE DEAD?

Last month, I dreamt of my birth father, something that has never happened before. The fact that my birth dad is deceased and I never met him makes the dream even more significant. Since the reverie, I've been noodling why he appeared to me and why now.

Under the plastic sheet of my desk blotter is a 3" × 3" headshot of my birth father. The genealogist who located him requisitioned the print from the university archives where my birth dad had been a tenured professor. The warm smile edging into his cheekbones, the full lips framing a distinctive smile, the glint of intelligence behind wire rims, and the gray threading through thinning reddish-gold locks are all fascinating details that greet me whenever I sit down to write.

During the four years that preceded my father's death, my two half-siblings attempted to soften my birth father's stance regarding "no contact"; they swore to me he might eventually come around and blamed his reluctance on his second wife, their stepmother. On what turned out to be the final attempt, my birth dad shut my brother down by saying, "Son, it's too complicated."

More disappointed than angry at my birth father, I have learned to accept his dismissal. He was and is entitled to his privacy. My goal in locating him had been to attain medical history, not to disrupt his life.

When my birth father died suddenly of a cardiac event in 2018, my sadness was more in commiseration with my half-siblings than it was for myself. They'd experienced a lifetime of memories with "our" father. Essentially, his role in my life had been that of a sperm donor. I believe that my lack of bitterness toward my birth dad is due to the meaningful relationship I shared with my adoptive father. In seeking out my birth father, I had never sought to replace Dad with another parent.

Ultimately, what I respect most about my birth father is his candor. His intentions were clear from the outset: here's the medical history you requested, and that's all I will provide. And I give him credit for providing it promptly. I'm acutely aware he could've ignored me completely.

My birth dad did me another favor. He disclosed my existence and whereabouts to his other children, my two half-siblings. Furthermore, he did not demand I refrain from contacting them. So, while I regret I never set eyes on my biological father, for all these reasons, I do not harbor ill feelings toward him. My biological father was out of my life as quickly as I knew his name, which leaves me puzzled as to why a man I'd given up on would make a premier appearance in my dreams on a Tuesday night at an airport hotel.

In my dream, a man resembling the headshot under my desk blotter paid a visit to me in my current home. He spent the night in my cozy guest room, and the next morning we lingered at the front door while he said his goodbyes. He enveloped me in a warm hug, smiled that notorious grin that my three siblings and I share, and then he was off. At this juncture in the dream, I remember vowing to phone my half-brother. I wanted him to know I had finally met "our father" and hosted him for an evening. My brother did not need to continue to nag "our father" to consider meeting me. It had happened.

I awoke with a clear recall of the dream's sequence. What's more? I was content, satisfied, happy. All was well. All was, in fact, perfect. Since launching my search, I'd met all the other key birth relatives in my family tree. Connecting with my birth dad completed the list. But when the gray hotel carpeting came into focus and I realized my birth dad's warm, reassuring hug had not occurred in this reality, questions stormed in.

Was the vision some sort of regret begging to be recognized? Was it an unrealized wish? Or was it a visit from a man who wanted me to know he did care about me, had wanted to meet me, and had wished he had done so before his sudden death?

Of course, I will never know the purpose of my birth dad appearing in my dream, but I have a theory. I am a highly sensitive person. I'm receptive. I have a history of connecting with others on different planes, levels, and realities. While the conscious part of my mind feels cheated that my biological father's visit had not occurred in this reality, the subconscious part of my brain assures me it happened. Because a dream hangover persists, I believe that my birth dad's energy is still present. And I feel better. Part of the other half of my *primal wound* is healing.

MISTAKES AND FORGIVENESS

When I was a kid, our family rules were simple: come home when the streetlights go on; don't hit your siblings; don't talk back to adults; finish all the food on your plate; and admit when you're wrong. While this list is not necessarily in order of importance, what my parents expected of my five siblings and me was abundantly clear: do the right thing. And, what happened if we got caught screwing up was also predictable: Say you're sorry and do everything you can to make it right.

My twin sister and I were eleven when the neighbors who lived three houses down moved out of state. Their house had not been well-maintained; therefore, it didn't sell right away. The property was vacant for most of the summer, and my sister, a friend, and I began to use it as our playground. We practiced cheerleading stunts and batted the volleyball around in the seclusion of their side yard. One thing led to another, as things tend to do with curious kids. We discovered an unlatched basement window on the south side of the house.

On a dare—no doubt with the promise of a prized treat like a yard of bubblegum or box of Lemonheads—one of us squeezed through the narrow casement window, dropped to the basement floor, and began to explore. Initially, the other two remained outdoors on lookout duty for the mailman, realtor, or nosy neighbor next door. The following day, a different one of us braved skimming through the narrow window and sliding to the concrete floor.

By the following week, we threw caution to the wind. With no one on the lookout, our trio cavorted through the vacated property, exploring every room on every floor. We peeked in dirty cupboards and dusty closets, noting the heaps of abandoned furnishings and belongings. We left everything as we found it. Our mission was one of curiosity, not destruction or thievery. We commended ourselves on our bravery. The experience was exhilarating.

While crawling out the window, one of us lost our footing and a shoe careened into the windowpane. To our horrified ears, the sound of shattering glass seemed to reverberate throughout the neighborhood. We huddled in the side yard, mulling our options, when a sedan pulled into the driveway. With our escape route effectively cut off, we grabbed our cheer stuff and volleyball, then walked sheepishly toward the realtor and the home's new owners. One of us offered the couple an apology for playing ball in their yard, and another pointed out the window we broke. We remained mute about our unsolicited explorations of their new house.

In the end, we fessed up to our parents, pooled our allowance money, and paid for the broken glass. The recompense was a relief compared to the admission of wrongdoing. I suppose because we were honest and earnest, my sister and I were asked numerous times to babysit for our new neighbor's children. To this day, my mother nurtures an ongoing friendship with those neighbors.

As children, it was common enough to make mistakes; we were expected to learn from them. But as adults, it's often hard to admit our errors, especially if the blunder affects others' safety or well-being. I made one of those silly email boo-boos the other day. I'd intended to forward an email and my pithy response to a like-minded friend, but instead, all of it went to the original sender. I'm still blushing with shame. It was a careless deed, and I spent the better part of an afternoon backtracking, explaining, and apologizing. And as I did this, the childhood escapade I shared above came immediately to mind. Lessons we learn in our formative years are strong and lasting.

Acknowledging that we are imperfect creatures is one thing. Seeking absolution is the second part of righting a wrong. Yet, why is it that forgiving ourselves is much harder than waiting for others to exonerate us?

FAVORITE SON, FAVORITE DAUGHTER

I've been thinking about favorites lately: favorite place to vacation (once COVID is officially vanquished, of course!) . . . favorite restaurant to nab a longed-for reservation (after my second shot this week) . . . and the favorite outfit I'll yank out of the back of the closet to wear to that much-anticipated evening out. We all have favorite things, places, and activities, but what about people? As I dwell on this, a story comes to mind.

I'm not certain when the family jest originated. If I had to guess, it probably began when my youngest daughter was in the primary grades and the older three kids—two daughters and a son—were in or about to enter high school. The six-year gap between the baby of the family and the next oldest meant I spent a lot of time toting her around to the older kids' activities.

To keep "the baby" occupied while I cheered for her siblings at the pool, baseball field, or basketball court, I packed a tote bag with coloring books, markers, special toys, and treats. If she was engaged or satisfied, I could relax and enjoy the older kids' endeavors.

Somewhere in time, one of my older kids must have muttered, "She's so spoiled." As kids do, another one tagged onto that comment with, "Yeah, she's Mom's favorite."

While I could have ignored this, the comment hit me wrong. I protested, "She's not my favorite. I don't play favorites." I believe those words, right down to my shoelaces.

Grinning wickedly, my son would have looked at one of his two older sisters and then sneered in my direction, "Well, if that's true, how come she gets everything she wants?"

"He's got a point, Mom," my middle daughter joined in. "You do give her everything she wants."

I bristled. "Perhaps I do appease her more than I should, but with good reason. If she's miserable at your games, she'll make everyone around us miserable. If she's happy, everyone's happy."

The knowing grins the kids tossed at one another meant they believed they were right.

Hands on my hips and voice raised, I said, "Making someone happy doesn't mean they're your favorite."

Much to my annoyance, at dinner that night my son and middle daughter resurrected the youngest-is-your-favorite argument again.

As my husband passed the carrots to my son, his brown eyes twinkled. "That's funny. I would have thought you were the favorite!" Everyone laughed.

"Well, I was the favorite until she came along," my son said, pointing to his blond-haired, pig-tailed sister. Smiling, he elbowed her, indicating that his words were a well-meaning tease.

The youngest took this all in. Her hazel eyes ping-ponged from her brother to her sisters, then back to my husband and me. When the carrots made their way to her end of the table, she set the platter down.

Staring at her brother, she declared, "Well, at least you know you will always be the favorite son. There's only one of you!"

"Ho-ho. She got you," my husband guffawed.

"Good one," my oldest daughter said, patting the youngest on her back.

As a mother, I believe it's important to set the record straight, especially when it concerns fairness. "I've been thinking about this 'favorite' thing since it started earlier today. Just so you know, on any given day any one of you might be my favorite. Just depends on what you've said or how you act."

"Amen to that," my husband added, winking at me.

A week or so later, I picked up a message on the kitchen answering machine from my middle daughter. "Hey, Mom! It's your favorite daughter. I'm at Kaitlin's house. I'll call you if I need a ride."

Not to be outdone, the next time the oldest daughter called she said, "Mom, favorite daughter here. Swim practice got over early, and I found a ride. See you soon!"

For years now, all four of my children have left similar messages on my voicemail, reminding me that on that day because of their good behavior, they believe they earned the right to be called "the favorite." Just hearing them say it pastes a smile on my face.

At Christmastime several years ago, I was perusing the internet for gift ideas, and I happened upon the ideal present for all four kids. I could hardly wait for Christmas morning. I waited until the other gift opening was complete, and then I handed each of them a package adorned in identical wrap and ribbons.

"Okay, everybody! Open them at the same time. Ready, set, go," I cheered.

"Oh, look, it's a pretty pink robe," the youngest said as she patted the soft fabric.

"Mine's black," said my son.

"Pull them out of the box and try them on," I commanded.

I could hardly wait to see their expressions as they noticed the embroidering on the back of the robes. One said, "Favorite Son," and the other three, "Favorite Daughter."

"Who's the favorite?" may have started as gentle ribbing for a mom who tried to make her kid happy, but the expression has morphed into a lingering, favorite family joke. For now, I have garnered the last word.

CAPTURING CANDID MOMENTS

I set my grandson down inside his pack-'n-play and ran for my cellphone with the fancy built-in camera. In gray sweatpants and a blue-striped onesie, he looked adorable. He'd woken from a solid nap, cheerful and content. As we strolled from his nursery to the kitchen, he gifted me with a string of small smiles, followed by what appeared to be a sincere attempt to coo—a true milestone requiring immediate documentation. As I shared the video clip via text with his working parents, I appreciated the ease with which current technology allowed me to capture such a momentous breakthrough.

When I was a young girl, on special occasions my dad dragged out and erected the equipment and accouterments that were a precursor to video technology. Setting up the contraption to make home movies occurred in dangerous chaos: at dawn among dried pine needles, paper wrappings, and half-assembled Christmas gifts; behind a dining room table strewn with a myriad of small, flimsy bowls of vinegar, food dye, and slippery hard-boiled eggs; or backed up against the gas range for a wide-angle shot of my five siblings and me wielding serrated knives and handfuls of slippery seeds and gooey pumpkin pulp.

A key component of Dad's home-movie paraphernalia was a tripod: not the plastic fold-up kind you find on Amazon today, but something more like a metal extension ladder. The second

major piece of equipment was a black-painted length of 2 ×
4 on which five bulbs the size of salad plates were mounted.
These items lived in the bowels of our dark, unfinished
basement behind cartons of holiday decorations, clothing,
and memorabilia. As Dad dragged the equipment upstairs, he
scraped or dinged the staircase walls, letting loose a resounding
"dammit-to-hell." Once the tripod and lighting were wrangled,
Dad connected everything via a tangle of thick, black cords to a
gray metal projector that spun a reel of fragile, silver 8mm film.

In testing the viability of the bulbs, invariably Dad burned
himself. Whether the body part affected was a finger, a forearm, or
the back of an arm, the startling, blistering pain sparked another
wave of curses. By the time the movie contraption was ready to
roll, everyone's nerves had frayed to the point of mass hysteria.

Dad was nearly undone by the retrieving-heaving-burning
routine, by the cacophony of our annoyed moans as we held
frozen grins or re-enacted the candid moments he had missed,
and by my mother's ministrations ("Are you okay, dear?") and
her pleas to hurry up. When the bulbs finally gave out with
a pop and a bright flash, our young eyes sustained a dizzying
blindness that seemed to last for hours. To my young mind,
capturing idyllic family moments on camera was tedious and
torturous.

Until Dad passed away, the candid moments he struggled
to collect lay forgotten and neglected in a storage locker. I
discovered the 8mm films in the bottom of a dusty, dilapidated
cardboard box. I paid heartily to have them converted to DVD,
but the results were somewhat disappointing. Early home
movies lacked sound and color, and the film's tissue-like fragility
produced grainy, often indiscernible images. The only thing

that brought Dad's stockpile to life was viewing them with my siblings and sharing our collective memories.

The difference between the home movies my father compiled and what current technology allows is obvious and profound. A single device, needing only an occasional charge, serves as a still camera, a video camera, and a communication portal. No hot set of bulbs, extension cord, or fragile film is required. Today the only physical effort required to set up a video is lifting an arm, pressing a button, and scrolling through contacts to select recipients. Swearing is not necessary. Posing and posting time is minimal. Color is the default, and blurry images are mostly a thing of the past.

I admire my father's tenacity and my mother's encouragement in creating the family movies of my childhood, and I appreciate the simplicity that today's technology affords me in sharing my grandson's antics.

I hope today's parents preserve and hand down their cell-phone videos, and that these collective memories debut in some new medium at future family events. Because who are we, and what are we, without our memories and loved ones to share them with?

TWO FATHERS, ONE DAD

In September 2017, my dad, known as "Chief" to most of us, succumbed to cancer. Dad left behind my mother, whom he had been married to for sixty-four years, my four siblings and me, our spouses, and a slew of grandkids. Dad loved all of us fiercely, he loved us gently, and he loved us with laughter and silliness. He loved us with his time.

Second to his family, Chief adored sports. Dad always had a book nearby, rocked the Scrabble board, and enjoyed a bowl of ice cream every night after dinner—heavy on the chocolate sauce and whipped cream. If there was a lineup of potential dads from which to pick, you would select Chief.

In May 2018, the heart of an eighty-two-year-old man in western Illinois seized suddenly and stopped functioning. Five days passed before his progeny were notified of his passing. I never met this man, my biological father, but because of him I have a curious mind and a parade of freckles. I wasn't given the chance to call him anything—father, Chuck, or sperm donor—because he refused to acknowledge me.

To his credit, my birth father provided me with several vital things: a complete medical history, a younger brother and sister, and the gift of life. All of which I treasure. I hold no ill feelings toward this other father, but I would have enjoyed laying eyes on him. His sudden death was a door closing, a dashed hope. It is a loss of a different magnitude and on a different scale than the grief I feel for the loss of the father who raised me. Mostly, I mourn my birth father's fleeting role in my life. There was much I had wanted to know about him, say to him, and ask him.

At the core of adoption is the severing of relationships, rejection, and denial. Adoption is also about being wanted, feeling loved, and finding belonging.

As we near Father's Day, I think about my two fathers and my one dad. I reflect on how the love I knew from Dad fills me with belonging, and how his benevolence and goodness dull the ache I feel over the absence of my biological father. Closed adoption restricted my ability to know my other father. If he had welcomed me into his life, he'd have found that my heart is big enough to love two fathers.

And so, at this special time of year, I acknowledge the two men who have influenced my life. While there is only one man that I call Dad, I cared about both of my fathers.

MY MOTHER'S WORDS

I hug my mother hard. In our lingering embrace, I notice that Mom's perky, salt-and-pepper bob has become a cap of bluish-white, and the pink skin at the part is more evident than I recall. I'm reluctant to pull free, so my fingers massage the sweet spot between her stooped shoulders.

"It's been too long," I say, and she lifts a warm palm to my cheek.

Mom doesn't need to say another word—her satisfied smile says it all: We made it through "the year like no other," and now it's safe to celebrate.

I situate my eighty-eight-year-old mother into the passenger seat of my Tahoe and help her locate the seatbelt receptacle. Sliding into the driver seat, I squeeze her hand, quieting a fresh batch of benign tremors that crop up without warning.

Mom quizzes me, "Where are we going, dear?"

I start to answer, but she waves off my reply, chuckling. "Never mind. It doesn't matter. What's important is that after all these months, we're healthy and together."

During the pandemic-prescribed months of social isolation, I talked to my memory-challenged mother nearly every day. Mostly, I called to entertain her with my children's and grandkids' latest escapades, but sometimes I phoned just to hear her voice. From our conversations, I assessed the impact of the quarantine on her morale and knew when I should rally my siblings to give her an extra boost. And by reading Mom's voice, I assured myself that she was still healthy, and the dreaded virus had not infiltrated her tiny apartment.

Of course, my over-zealous efforts hadn't fooled Mom. "Oh, honey. You mustn't worry about me so much. I'm well cared for by the assisted living staff. If, and when, I get the virus is up to 'the powers that be.'"

When Mom muttered, "the powers that be," I giggled. My amusement had nothing to do with COVID-19 or the capable senior living staff. "The powers that be" is a well-worn phrase of my mother's.

When my five siblings and I were growing up, Mom used "the powers that be" to satisfy our angst surrounding a myriad of uncertainties. Like whether I'd make the cheerleading squad. Or whether the gathering thunderstorms would rain out my brother's baseball playoff game. For the longest time, I thought "the powers that be" must be a corps of unnamed saints charged with handling questionable circumstances or challenging situations.

As an adult, I realize my mother uses this saying to explain away the unknowable or to end difficult conversations. While Mom's expression is not much different than my favorite catchphrase—"let's just see how this plays out"—my mother's words, "the powers that be," possess a soothing, mystical quality. It suggests a higher power keeps tabs on the events in our lives. And something about this adage is more appealing than my nebulous go-to response: *let's just see.*

"Here's the restaurant, Mom," I say, pointing to the nondescript building anchoring a strip center.

As the two of us navigate the potholed parking lot, hand in hand, we chat about the history of the bistro I chose for our first post-vaccine reunion dinner. When my folks were raising our family of six, a dinner out at Johnny's Italian was a treat that happened only once in a great while. Usually, Grandma Mimi instigated the excursion and picked up the tab, too.

At the check-in counter, Mom fiddled with the strap of her handbag while I leaned in and whispered to the hostess, confirming our party of four.

Above her wire-rimmed glasses, my mom's gray eyebrows arched. "Who's joining us?" she asked.

My eyes crinkled with the idea of surprising her. "You'll just have to wait and see."

While my mother might remember that my son and his girlfriend planned to move into the neighboring village, due to the pandemic's need to continually reorder our lives, Mom has lost track of the timing. While Mom studied the familiar Italian menu, my son's large frame loomed tableside. Stooping over his grandmother, Danny consumed her shoulders in a hug, and then he planted a loud smack on her beaming face. Mom's pleasure at seeing yet another family member tickled my insides.

"Remind me where the house is again, honey?" Mom asked Danny.

"Just a few blocks from here, Grandma. A ten-minute walk from you!"

When Dan explained all of this, Mom marveled at how the next generation had landed within a few miles of the home where my folks raised my five siblings and me. As my son and his girlfriend updated my mother on their jobs and their ideas to decorate and landscape their new home, another one of my mom's favorite phrases popped into my head: "Remember where you come from."

Of course, it's not hard to remember where you come from when your mother and son live within minutes of your childhood house and stomping grounds. But whenever my mother uttered these words to my sisters and brothers, her intent was not for us to take her literally. No, we all knew from Mom's raised voice, cautionary tone, and pointer finger fiercely stabbing the stale kitchen air that she was prompting us to keep in mind the values she strove to ingrain. To be respectful, courteous, and kind. To be humble, generous, and grateful. To give without expectation and to ask forgiveness when we'd committed a wrong.

Quite simply, "remember where you come from" means wherever you go and whatever you do, be the person I have taught you to be.

As I watched my son interact with his only living grandparent, I reflected upon the challenges of the past year. I'm not surprised Mom weathered all of it as she did. While I can attribute some of Mom's luck in evading the virus to "the powers that be," her survival has more to do with her attitude and values. My parents' generation understood delayed gratification, deemed frugality a virtue, and believed saving for a rainy day would have a meaningful payoff. They worked hard and lived by the strong values they imparted. And family was everything to them. I took all of this to heart in raising my family and hope I did as good a job as my folks.

As Mother's Day nears, I'm grateful. I'm thankful the virus spared my mother's life and that we can add this celebration to the rich bank of family memories. And I'm appreciative: for the well of meaning behind my mother's pet phrases; for the strong core values she and Dad imparted to my siblings and me; and for the opportunity to gather with three generations of family. I can't think of a better way for the next generation to glean wisdom from my mother's words.

WHAT DO YOU WANT?

My husband and I went out for dinner recently with people I've gotten to know through my Catholic Charities post-adoption support group. When the waiter approached our table, my fellow adoptee was immersed in sharing an update about the search for her birth mother.

We stopped chattering when the waiter asked, "Has everyone had enough time with the menus?"

When we nodded, the waiter turned to my husband. "Sir, I'll start with you. What do you want?"

Perhaps it was the details of my friend's turbulent adoption search. Or it could have been the events of the week that had just wrapped up. I'd spent most of it speaking to book clubs and guesting on podcasts to discuss my adoption search experience and my recently released memoir, *Twice a Daughter.* As much as I truly enjoyed these events, as a functioning introvert I was drained.

In retrospect, I believe that the combined effects of back-to-back events, deep conversations, and the waiter's query *What do you want?* are what triggered the memory I share now.

It was April 2012. My twin sister and I were six months into a blissful reunion with our birth mother. The previous fall, my confidential intermediary had brokered an agreement with her:

exchange letters and photographs through the CI's office, and then decide if you desire further contact.

Three exchanges of notes and precious photos led to our first phone call, followed by an emotion-packed in-person meeting with my birth mom, my twin sister, and me. The months following the first birthdays we celebrated together were consumed with more phone calls and exchanges of notes containing old photographs and family genealogy.

I was fifty-two. I had spent most of my life wondering about my first mother and why she had placed us for adoption. Now that she had finally welcomed us into her life, I was giddy with joy. Content and complete, I marveled at how far we'd come and speculated about what was still possible.

As was my way during that early stage of our reunion, I picked up the landline most mornings and punched in my birth mom's home phone number. I wanted to hear her voice and learn what she was up to for the day. She answered after a few rings, and a brilliant smile lit my face. Butterflies danced in my belly like the ones a teenage girl feels when calling a new boyfriend.

After a few moments of chit-chat, there was a pause on the line, and then my birth mom blurted out, "What do you want?"

Her words stunned me. Breath hitched in my chest. Wasn't it obvious what I wanted? Didn't she want the same things I wanted: to learn everything about each other and the lives we had led, be magnanimously welcomed into each other's extended family, and forge a mother–daughter bond to replace the one that had been severed?

I closed my eyes and stammered, "I just want . . . to have a relationship with you."

Certainly, my mother's direct manner was off-putting, but it was more than that. I was disappointed, deflated. I wanted her to have intuited what I desperately sought. As my biological mother, I had expected her to instinctively know that I had always wanted her in my life, that I needed to know everything about her, not just why she had placed us for adoption. I wanted her to not just fill in the gaps in my identity; I wanted to belong to her and for her to belong to me.

Putting words around all this because she demanded it facilitated several outcomes. Her question pierced our reunion bubble. It pushed my eager-beaver attitude aside and effectively set me on guard. Doubt and misunderstanding seeped into our relationship. And my mother's "What do you want?" caused me to readjust my inflated expectations.

I realized I had been misguided in believing our shared genes meant we would instantly understand one another. I supposed the unique bond I have with my identical twin sister had set me up to assume this—Jen and I are rarely out of step with one another. And I understood that while our reunion meant I was getting to know my mother, I was limited to how far she would allow me in.

Birth moms from my parents' generation were subjected to systemic societal shame. Because of the disgrace of unwed pregnancy, women were often shunned by friends and disowned by family. Many birth mothers will go to their deathbeds safeguarding their painful secrets.

"What do you want?" As off-putting as the question was, I now understand why my birth mom asked it. She had spent her entire adult existence presenting herself so that others would not think less of her. I can imagine that might have made her suspicious of everyone, including family members like long-lost birth daughters. That simple question—*What do you want?*—is posed daily by waiters, salespeople, strangers, and family members.

We don't always know what we want, do we? Sometimes it's easy to decide. Should I have the chicken parmesan or the eggplant? But understanding people and discerning how best to reconcile our wants and their needs takes time.

I'm still in reunion with my birth mom. I talk to her every few weeks. Our relationship has evolved into one much like I enjoyed with my favorite Aunt Ginger. And, while I do not always know exactly how to please my birth mother, I treasure the day that she reentered my life.

FELLOWSHIP AND FAVORITE
FAMILY PHRASES

The other night as another magnificent summer sunset faded, a few members of my family and me—the same ones I've been sequestered with since early spring—lingered in our sunroom over beverages. We were weary of the tumultuous news and of Netflix. We sought fellowship. I'm not sure how it started, but we began to rattle off old stories from when the kids were little. One story led to another, and what emerged was a list of memorable sayings specific to our family's experiences.

No doubt your family has its set of quirky, inside-joke-kind-of-phrases, too—those witty or moving one-liners uttered innocently (or not) that, over time, have become standard vocabulary and family legend.

Here are a few highlights from my family's list.

It was the Fourth of July, and our oldest daughter had recently learned to ride her two-wheeler—just in time to take part in the annual town parade. Like all the other neighborhood kids, the day before the event she threaded red, white, and blue crepe paper through the bike spokes, and then pushed streamers into the ends of her handlebars. The morning of the parade, she was out in the driveway before breakfast practicing pedaling and braking.

July Fourth that year, like most, July Fourths in the Chicago area, was hot and steamy. If Mother Nature had provided any cooling lake breezes, they must have been freshening folks on a different Great Lake. The sun was high and bright, and it had the sky all to itself. It was a real scorcher—a day for popsicles, hats, and plenty of sunscreen.

Our family claimed a spot along the parade route, and my husband walked our little gal over to the starting area adjacent to the fire station. He got her lined up alongside some pals, kissed her good luck, and turned to leave. Her big brown eyes begged him to walk the parade route beside her. The first few blocks were in direct sunlight and uphill. Sweat trickled from her scalp and dampened the festive ribbons tied on her ponytails. Undeterred, she pedaled hard. She focused on the road ahead of her, muttering to herself. Her dad leaned in and caught the words she was whispering: *I think I can. I think I can.* He chuckled at the infamous refrain from *The Little Engine That Could.* That fledgling bicyclist is now a mother herself, and that four-word sentence, *I think I can*, remains a favorite family battle cry.

The same determined young girl who pedaled the length of that sweltering July Fourth parade coined the next memorable quip.

In raising our four kids, I admit that we tended to spoil them. We threw elaborate birthday parties. Each child had their own room. They were gifted with the latest toys and wore trendy clothes. Not only did we enroll them in a multitude of activities and sports, but we also hauled them everywhere. To the pool. To a friend's house. To the lake with friends for sleepover weekends. Perhaps you're guilty of the same indulging behavior.

During those child-rearing years, my husband and I had a standing agreement. One day out of the weekend, I got to sleep in, and he took the troops for breakfast. I'm not certain how he learned of the M&M Restaurant (sadly, it's no longer in business), but it was the hands-down family favorite. Who wouldn't like chocolate ice cream shakes, pancakes, or waffles with rich maple syrup for breakfast? And with that much sugar coursing through their systems, before the outing was over, at least one overfed child was obnoxiously twitchy, feisty, and/or whiny.

My husband is not one to hold back on calling a kid up short.

"Hey, what's your problem? After all that we've done today, I can't believe you're going to act like that. When I was a kid, five of us lived in a tiny house with only one bathroom. You kids are so spoiled."

I can see his face reddening, and his hands thrown up in disgust.

Little smarty pants, alias sweaty biker chick, thought about this. As the oldest, she took it upon herself to become the group's spokesperson. Putting her hands on her hips, she glared at him. "Dad, we did not spoil ourselves!"

What does a dad say to that?

Nothing. He laughed, and so did the few M&M patrons who were within earshot. Now and again that wisecrack comes back to haunt my husband. "Hey Dad, 'member how we didn't spoil ourselves . . . do you think you can help me out with xxx?" Sometimes that little nostalgic jest is enough to tease the wallet open.

One more anecdote before I close. The youngest of our four was always dragged to her older siblings' events. She and I would pull out coloring books and crayons on the bottom bleacher at Little League games. At her sister's basketball games, her backpack was loaded with bead kits and troll dolls. When we'd get home, tired and hungry, she'd drag all her favorite toys and crafts back inside.

On one of those nights, she exploded with frustration. "Mommy, I can't open the door. I'm too full of hands."

Since then, any time a few of us are together and loaded down with gear or groceries, "I'm full of hands" is thrown out with a giggle.

Family and fellowship. Memories and nostalgia. Wisecracks and one-liners. They're such nice diversions from the anxiety and worries that occupy our daily lives. With the future still uncertain due to COVID-19 and its variants, shore yourself up with whatever goodies you've stockpiled as families.

PLANTING TULIPS

For me, fall has always meant putting the summer garden to bed and digging in tulips, daffodils, and hyacinths for early spring color. On a recent trip to Amsterdam, I made a point of visiting the Keukenhof Gardens. The elaborate landscapes and colorful beds of tulips were magnificent and inspirational. Years ago, when my thumb was its darkest green, every October I planted bushels of bulbs grown in Holland. Now, when autumn whistles in or I glimpse mass plantings of tulips, I chuckle to myself—not because I miss the rigorous process of selecting and planting bulbs, but because of something that happened decades ago when my tulips woke from their wintry slumber.

Farming is in my blood. While I did not grow up harvesting corn, I have always had a garden, which has varied in size and scale depending on the size of my yard. The Dutch tulip catalogs were like gold to me in those peak gardening years. I'd dog-ear the pages, circle my favorites, then pop my order in the mail. When October rolled in, packets of bulbs found their way from the garage and into my yard for planting.

While I lived in an old Victorian on the main street of town, tulips produced the memory I'm about to share. The flower borders in my compact front yard were full and flourishing, so I expanded my scope. The concrete driveway to the right of the house needed sprucing up, I thought. To soften the edges of the hardscape, I envisioned a vibrant wave of spring color.

Tulips!

Scouring my catalogs, I ordered early- and late-blooming bulbs in various stem heights and colors. When autumn arrived and the kids were in school, I donned my elbow-length gardening gloves and dug in neat rows of tulips along the driveway by the neighbor's fence. I placed markers in the mounds of soil so in the spring I'd know what varieties bloomed.

Once the winter snow cover melted, I began monitoring my driveway bulbs' progress. By April, green sprouts emerged from the mulch. The regular spring rains had produced stems, sturdy and strong. The vibrant oranges, dazzling pinks, and gripping purples were staged to open with the next warm-up.

I was standing at the kitchen sink when I spied my preschooler escape the fenced-in yard with our old collie. Even though it was close to ten in the morning, my son was still in his favorite Superman pajamas. Some days it wasn't worth the hassle to get him changed out of those. I don't recall if the matching cape with its Velcro strips was attached, but I suspect it was on the family room carpet. Sometimes, as you fly around the house mimicking your idols, a cape can get in the way.

Before I could reach the back door, my son had picked up a stick from the driveway. Before I could skip down the back steps, my angel had karate-chopped the first row of tulips. Before I unlatched the gate, he was on to the second row. And before he lifted the weapon for the assault on the final grouping, I swatted the stick from his pudgy fist. He had been so dedicated to the superhero task of taking out the enemy in Mommy's driveway that he hadn't heard my vicious protests.

As I came to a gasping standstill, my boy's chubby cheeks glistened with tears. He'd been battling good and evil with his dog. My tirade had scared him silly. I realized my error. I hadn't warned my son about how important it was to his mommy to see all the flowers open their colorful faces. I hadn't asked him to leave them alone. I hadn't thought to do so. I had simply planted my bulbs in the fall and waited for spring to do its magic.

I looked at the shorn flowers and my son's sorrowful face.

I said, "Go ahead. Finish the job. Make sure you get all the bad guys."

As my budding superhero completed his mission, I reasoned that a fully shorn garden was more appealing from the curb than a spotty hatchet job.

I loved viewing the expansive tulip displays at Keukenhof Gardens. My pleasure was multi-faceted. Because of my love of gardening, I enjoyed the unusual varieties, colors and textures, the showy scale of the garden, and the way pockets of bulbs enhanced mature spring beds. And of course, the Holland tulips brought back with vivid reality that scene with my young son in the driveway: the morning when he annihilated the enemy with the swat of a stick.

Fall is a special time to prepare for winter and to plan for spring growth, and it is a time to remember. While gardens make us happy, memories make us happiest.

TWO LESSONS LEARNED

Friday is our day. I pick up DJ, my two-year-old grandson, around 8:30, and our first stop is the drive-thru window at the local coffee shop.

As we wait our turn in the serpentine line of cars, I twist around the Tahoe's bulky headrest and ask DJ, "Would you like milk or apple juice today?"

"Cake pop," he shouts. His chubby legs kick wildly at the passenger seat back.

I stifle a laugh. "OK. Cake pop. Do you want milk, too?"

"Juice, Yu-Yu! Juice!"

DJ is still working on his "L's." My fear is that when I'm a shriveled-up, ninety-seven-year-old lady in a nursing home, I'll still be known as "Yu-Yu." And, at that final stage in life, nobody will know how my Gramma name morphed from "Lulu" to "Yu-Yu."

I inch the car closer to the ordering kiosk. "OK, DJ, your Lulu will get you an apple juice and a cake pop."

I make a mental note: After our usual stops at the car wash and the post office, DJ and I had better head to the beach or pool so my little guy can run off the potent sugar buzz I'm about to pay handsomely for.

At the gas station, DJ watches me from his car seat as I pump gas. I wave to him through the open car window, and he waves back. After I snag the receipt for the express car wash attached to the service station, I replace the pump handle and open my car door.

"Close the door, Yu-Yu. 'Member?"

DJ doesn't mean the driver's side door. He is reminding me to close the little round door that hides the gas cap. As I do so, I chuckle at myself and at DJ's perceptiveness.

When I put the car in gear, DJ's voice is louder than it needs to be. "Mask off, Yu-Yu! Mask off."

I know what my daughter would want me to say: "DJ, use your inside voice, please. Ask me again in a nice way." But I don't say that. I throw my hot-pink mask on the console and smile knowingly around the headrest at DJ.

My grandson and I have done this fill-the-car-with-gas-and-go-through-the-car wash drill a half-dozen times. I know. There's anxiety building up in him. The machinations of the car wash fascinate and intrigue him. Thrill him. But the combination of the flood of bubbles, which obscures the view, and the dramatic thud-thud of the rinse cycle challenges him. DJ's insistent tone is less about him being leery of a mask—one that makes his "Yu-Yu" look less like his grandmother—and more about struggling to control the cocktail of fear-joy brimming up inside his little body.

At the entrance to the car wash, I enter the code off the receipt and pull forward. As we wait for the green light go-ahead, DJ's voice shifts to a whisper.

"Hold hand, Yu-Yu. Hold hand!" he says.

The first time we navigated this car wash routine together, I was puzzled by DJ's sudden show of anxiety. Then, I quickly clicked out of my seat belt and threaded an outstretched palm through the seats. As the car lurched into the wash chamber, DJ clutched my long fingers in his small ones and fixed a steely gaze at the windshield. When I returned DJ home at dinnertime, I quizzed his dad.

"Just a little anxiety, but it didn't mean he didn't enjoy it," my son-in-law verified.

Beautiful, I thought. My grandson had the sense to express his need for a soothing touch so he could experience something in which he was profoundly interested.

Whether you are a child, a teenager, or an adult, I offer two takeaways from my day with DJ. If you succumb to unhealthy demands, like ordering cake pops and apple juice, make sure you have certain countermeasures planned. And remember that, oftentimes, joyful moments come from conquering some amount of fear.

For me, a day with DJ means enacting a relaxed agenda, regarding the world with a finer focus, and appreciating the resulting magic. The time we spend together is not without moments of frustration, a few tears, and tests of will, but there also is laughter and inspiration. Each Friday I spend with my grandson is a marvelous contrast and a reset compared to the six other days when I'm forced to experience our crazy world as an adult.

WHY DO WE BLAME?

Have you noticed there is more blame passed around than there is praise?

The president repeatedly says, "the virus out of China," refusing to refer to it with the appropriate scientific label: COVID-19. I suppose there is a little part of all of us that blames China for what our nation went through.

But why is it that our first inclination when something goes wrong is to cast a wide net for someone or something to blame?

Perhaps it's a natural human tendency to shift the focus from oneself and heap it onto others. It might be that we need to lay blame to compensate for our lack of control. Experts say blaming provides a way of devaluing others, making the blamer feel superior. Seeing others as less worthwhile makes the blamer "perfect."

Most of us are guilty of blaming behavior. When battling to get at the secrets of my closed adoption, I hired an online search agency that took my money and did little else. I blamed myself first for being naïve and trusting, then I blamed the closed adoption system that protected the rights of my birth and adoptive parents over my right to know.

I blamed my adoptive mother often throughout my years-long search for my birth relatives. The first incident was when I dug out a small mistruth regarding my baptism. My baptismal certificate was issued by Holy Name Cathedral in Chicago, but it turned out that instead of receiving my first sacrament at the Cathedral, I'd been baptized in a little chapel at St. Vincent's Orphanage. My mother hadn't lied, but I blamed her for perpetuating a lie since she hadn't asked enough questions of the adoption agency.

The second major blaming episode I am guilty of is related to my being a twin. Catholic Charities told my mother that my sister and I were fraternal twins. A DNA test several years ago revealed that this is false. We are identical twins. Who should I blame for this lie: My mother, the nuns at the orphanage, the Department of Vital Records, the nurse at the maternity hospital where I was born? Any of them? All of them?

Why do I need to blame anyone?

I have been quite angry when discovering mistruths and misperceptions about my existence. Am I embarrassed about my blaming behavior? No. I acknowledge it as a human failing. Blaming gave me the vehicle for shifting powerful negative energy from myself and onto someone else. Could blaming behavior be considered a useful self-protection mechanism? Perhaps, but I have found over time that acceptance and forgiveness make me feel better about myself than does blaming others.

REJECTIONS AND COPING

In an article discussing COVID-19's lingering effects on the brain, Siddhartha Nadkarni, MD, assistant professor of neurology and psychiatry at NYU Langone, stated, "When the brain is injured it usually takes longer for those networks to get back online and recover."

In other words, the brain takes longer to heal than the rest of the body. And when it comes to hurts of the heart—wounds due to loss and rejection—the heart forgives long before the mind forgets. That brain of ours . . . it's a complicated organ. Besides memories, it holds onto physical injury and emotional suffering.

When it comes to rejection, there are "all kinds of kinds," to borrow a phrase from one of Miranda Lambert's songs. There are small hurts, medium-sized wrongs, and then the *big ones,* which tend to cause lingering damage.

Small rejections are minor slights such as an unreturned email or phone call, or a person who chooses not to greet you or forgets your name. These behaviors, while rude and disappointing, may be inadvertent or caused by other factors. Often these dings are eased with an apology or fade in importance with a good night's sleep.

Moderate hurts are a bit more painful: for example, a friend who betrays a confidence. Like minor slights, moderate hurts add to our armor of resiliency. While these negative incidents expose vulnerabilities and are demoralizing, we learn how to better handle the situation next time, and we move on.

The big rejections—losses and wounds that send us into a tailspin or counseling—are life-altering. Affairs. Divorce. A friend who for some unknown reason becomes an archrival or enemy. A birth parent who refuses to acknowledge you. These predicaments don't just cause us to lose sleep; they make us feel awful right down to our toes. Our wounded state can last for sustained periods. We find it difficult to cope, and we blame ourselves: I should have done xxx. I'm not good enough. We invent reasons why the hurt happened: it's because I did xxx, they know xxx about me, or I'm not xxx.

You know the drill.

When my birth mother denied my request for contact in 2010, I was devastated. Once the tears dried up, I was angry, and then the sadness returned. The yearning I'd had—to learn where I had come from and why she placed us for adoption—evaporated. I was in a bad place. Despite the compassion I received from family and friends, I needed professional advice. A social worker suggested my birth mother's dismissal might be due to circumstances in her current life. This reminded me that just because I was ready to find my birth mom didn't mean she was ready to be found.

Eventually, my birth mom did reach out. And years later, when my birth father rejected my contact, I reminded myself about the social worker's advice. It worked. When my birth dad dismissed me, I didn't sink into self-pity. Because of what had transpired with my birth mom, I hoped that someday he would change his mind, too.

Lambert's lyrics will always ring true. Indeed, there are all kinds of kinds. All kinds of people do all kinds of harm—whether deliberately or inadvertently—and there are all kinds of advice on how to cope with rejection and loss.

Here's what most experts suggest:

1. Acknowledge the pain and grieve the loss.
2. Don't blame yourself or take it personally.
3. Strengthen your resiliency.
4. Keep putting yourself out there.
5. Seek professional help if the symptoms don't lessen.

When it comes to coping with the effects of the pandemic on our bodies and psyches, time will tell. Dealing with rejection is even harder during a stressful event such as a pandemic. Until all the uncertainty plays out, I'll be utilizing that list of coping strategies and I will augment it with a sprinkling of inspiring music, a relaxing daily meditation, an invigorating daily walk, and a nice, chilled glass of rosé.

Section III

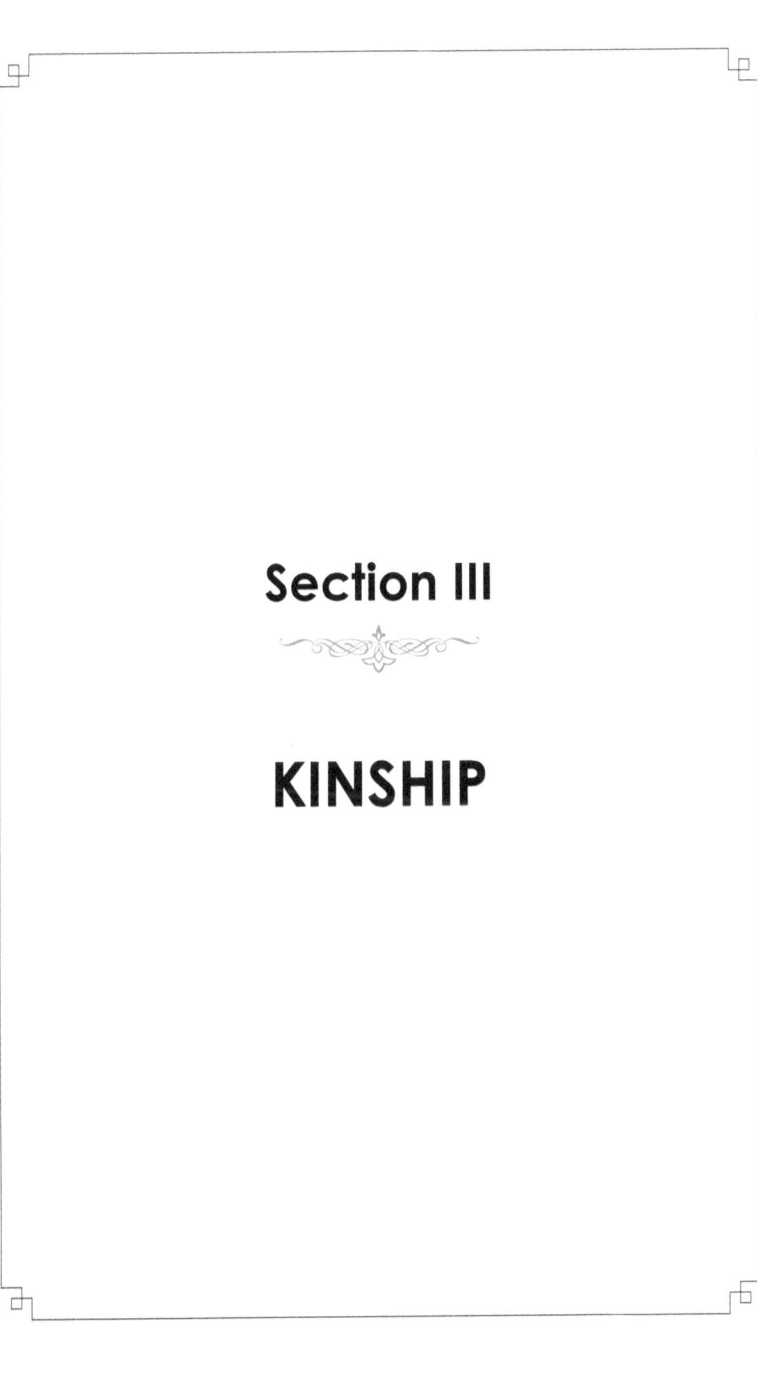

KINSHIP

A MOTHER IS NEVER FAR

Personal relationships can be difficult to foster in person. They're even harder when the people you hold dear are hundreds of miles away. Add a deathly pandemic and potentially dangerous air travel to the mix, and maintaining long-distance relationships becomes über-challenging.

As heartened as I am to have Zoom and FaceTime as communication options during these troubled times, I'm equally grateful for the ability to walk outdoors! Walking is how I've coped with the many disruptions and inconveniences brought on by COVID-19, and almost always, something inspirational emerges from the time spent wandering on foot.

I logged a lot of miles during the shutdown. So, when the summer of 2020 began, I ordered a fresh pair of sneakers and splurged on a second set. Last week, when I climbed into the red Escort to drive my daughter back to her apartment in DC, my walking shoes were at the top of the suitcase. I planned to spend the night in DC with her, take a good morning walk, then continue to New Jersey to visit my other daughter and her family. The last time I held my new grandson was Leap Day weekend, two weeks before COVID-19 began ravaging the East Coast. He is now ten months old.

Jack and I sprawl out on his purple and orange play quilt, and I make a barricade of blocks, books, and stuffed animals around the two of us. It's anyone's guess whether this will thwart my grandson's manic curiosity about the air conditioning vent on the wall nearby. In yoga pants, a sports bra, and a tee, I am already dressed for our morning walk, on hold until my daughter Molly slips in from another long night as an OB/GYN resident. The few minutes Molly can spend with Jack each morning before sleeping and heading back to the hospital are like gold coins. First, Jack and I will play, then we will walk.

My hamstrings burn and my lower back tightens as I scoop up my exuberant grandson and plop him into my lap for another reading of *Goodnight Moon*. When I cuddle Jack, my chin hovers over his fine, golden hair, gifting me with a whiff of last night's scrub of baby shampoo. The combined nostalgia of the soap's familiar scent and the baby board book—one I read easily a thousand times to my four children—pulls on my heartstrings. I miss those days of mothering, and I resent the pandemic for preventing me from being active in my family's lives now. As I clear my throat and ready my voice for a moving rendition of Goodnight Moon, one that will hold Jack's attention, tires grind on the gravel drive and a car door shuts.

Before Jack and I can untangle ourselves, Molly blazes through the back door. She towers above us on the vibrant blanket, smiling and reaching for Jack. Fussing with her toddler, she quizzes me about what kind of night he had and whether I was successful in getting him to eat anything else with his "O's." I offer a glowing Gramma commentary while evaluating Molly's appearance. Her skin tone is as pale as the morning clouds that stream by, and the bluish-gray tinge below her lower lashes makes it look like she applied eyeshadow in the wrong place. Both are a barometer of how she's balancing work and family life. The irony of this "mother's mothering" moment is not lost on me. Molly's immediate concern is for her child. In turn, my focus is on my daughter's health and well-being.

Molly dances with the squirming Jack, and he giggles with obvious delight at his mother's entrée into our morning routine. As I gather the toys and books and stow them in the toybox, the pair stroll, cooing and squealing, into the adjacent dining room.

Halting in front of the picture window, Molly jabs a finger at the backyard. "Look, Jack. Mom! Come quick! Two deer are asleep in the grass."

Last evening and into the early morning hours, Tropical Storm Fay ambled through the greater New York/New Jersey area, dumping hail and enough rain to make a swamp of the side yard. The tempest also infused enough moisture into the heat-challenged grass to cause it to glow like a "light chrome green" Crayola.

Five feet apart, noses nuzzling into white underbellies, two fawns lie sleeping in the dewy, lime-green grass. Twins! Had it been a day earlier, their fur—the color of gingerbread—might have blended in with the dried-out lawn, and then we would have missed this spectacle.

As if the twin fawns sense an audience, they twitch, stretching legs so long and sinewy that we wonder how they can stand, much less possess the energy to outrun a predator. Star-shaped white spots freckle their light brown skins, telegraphing their age. Like Jack, the fawns are not quite a year. In another few months, the white spots will fade, and the fawns will be yearlings. Just like my grandson.

Jack shrieks, and the baby deer lift their heads in unison. Telescoping their ears around, the not-quite-yearlings scramble up, play peek-a-boo with us from behind the swing set, then dart off into the woods. Perhaps my grandson's squeal and wild movements spooked the deer, but another possibility is that their mother was feeding nearby and called out to them to join her. From my experience with the herds of deer populating the woods behind my summer house, I know a doe will deposit her young in a protected place and go off and feed. She is never far away, and she will always return. It occurs to me that I am like that with my family, despite obstacles like restricted air travel and pandemics.

"Awww. They're gone now. Wasn't that cool, Jack?" Molly beams at her son.

I head to the kitchen and pull out the eggs to make Molly an omelet. "Perhaps we'll catch another glimpse of the deer when Jack and I take our walk."

Scrambling eggs, I tell Molly about the fawn I happened upon during one of my walks before driving out to the East Coast.

I had gotten a late start, and the morning was already steamy. Instead of my usual route along the exposed lakefront, I scaled the narrow, shady lane behind the lake house. Once an old Potawatomi Indian path, Duneland Beach Road in northwest Indiana is now an asphalt-drenched two-lane street. Following its zig-zagging path, I breezed past scores of cozy summer cottages tucked neatly into forests of towering oak and pine. The route took me past the inn and community park, then whisked me deeper into the woods, away from the shoreline. Avoiding the last mile of road, one that would deposit me near the railroad tracks, I detoured into the neighboring community of Long Beach. By this time, my shirt was soldered to my shoulder blades, and I was rationing my water. When the old grammar-school-turned-community center appeared at the bottom of an incline, my exhalation became a pleased sigh.

I slowed my steps. Perhaps there was a water fountain on the playground where I could refill my water bottle.

In that pause of relief at seeing the old school and the hope of badly needed water, I studied the homes and yards around me like a potential buyer. I admired the muted color palette of the house on my left, the unique shutters of the house next door, and the flowerpots overflowing on the front steps. Doing so took my mind off the oppressive humidity, my thirst, and the sobering thought of a long trek home. The air was so stifling and stagnant that an afternoon thunderstorm was almost certain. Around me, nothing dared move. No bees were evident poking around the packed flowerbeds. A bird fluttered in a lush silver maple, only to reposition itself on a shadier branch. Only the hissing of cicadas and sprinklers reverberated in the thick air. I asked myself why I had ventured out on such a taxing day.

To my right, I detected motion. In a verdant bank of dune grass, several blades quivered. In the absence of morning breezes, I reasoned, something had to be in the thick reeds, making them rustle. Curious, I quieted my breath, stepped onto the pebbled parkway, and leaned into the massed plantings like a proper Peeping Tom. I had the eerie sensation of being watched. As I bent over, the trembling in the grass escalated. I sensed fear, and it was not mine.

My breath hitched. A few feet from my sneakers, the top of a soft brown head and one long, pointy ear were visible. A fawn was hidden in the dune grass. My body snapped up as if something from the garden had stung me. I did a 360 and scanned the street. Now, it was I who was afraid. The fawn's mother had to be close by. If the doe witnessed me trespassing on the spot where she had hidden her young, she might charge.

As I finish the retelling of summer's first "fawn in the grass" encounter, Molly's blue eyes widen. "Mom, what did you do? Did the mother appear?"

I chuckle. "No, I never saw the mom. I got out of there. Fast. But, when I got closer to the old school, I ran into a man pushing his son in a stroller. I warned him to be on the lookout for the doe. She would never leave her fawn for very long."

Molly hands Jack to me and rubs her eyes. "Time for my nap." From the counter, she picks up the baby's sippy cup and fills it with water. "Have a nice walk, you guys!"

We wave bye-bye, and I buckle my grandson into his all-terrain stroller. In the backyard, there is no sign of the twin fawns or the doe. "All right then, let's go, Jack. Off to Foote's Pond. Maybe the heron will be there today. For sure, we'll see some ducks paddling and hear that big old bullfrog's belch. Oh, the things we will see . . ."

The sound of the stroller's wheels crunching against the pavement drowns out the squeak of my sneakers. Our easy wandering lulls me into constructive thought. I think about my encounters with fawns in the grass, motherhood, mothering, and all the threats to relationships and life. What seems clear is that life prevails despite disease. It thrives right smack in front of us, despite all we do. That should teach us something. Give us hope.

Tomorrow, I will return to the summer house and leave my daughter and her family behind. My heart is not heavy. Even if the miles that separate us are many, a mother is never far from her young.

THE NURSING FAWN

Duneland Beach Road is an old Potawatomi Indian path drenched with asphalt. Crumbly patches mar its surface, caused in part by harsh winter storms and the sandy dune, which is its foundation. The road begins as an exit off Highway 20 near Notre Dame School, then jigs and jags around two hundred cottages, dense thickets, and forests of towering oak. It winds past the Duneland Beach Inn and the community park but never glimpses the Lake Michigan shoreline. In winter, one must pull into someone's driveway to allow another vehicle to pass cleanly. If this stretch of road were a piece of furniture you'd call it a chair-and-a-half, not a loveseat.

On this muggy July afternoon, the right tires of my youngest daughter's Ford Escort settle onto the shoulder of Duneland Beach Road. We are parked a few feet shy of the four-way stop that protects pedestrians laden with beach gear from the traffic that barrels down the ridge off Arrowhead Road. My daughter's car is motionless—not because we need to allow another vehicle to pass, nor to genuflect at the stop sign, but to indulge me in the picture I crave.

"Stop here. I want to get a shot of the fawn with its mother," I say.

"Oh, Mom. It's so cute. Looks at those spots. It's a baby." She coos, much like I imagine her doing when she becomes an aunt for the first time later this summer.

My daughter, a recent college graduate, will board a Southwest flight to Washington, DC before the weekend hits a crescendo. Her past life as a college coed is being supplanted by her new role as an asset manager for a REIT. The last of my four offspring to make her mark on an ever-changing global economy, she and I have soaked up these last few hours together. When I drop her at Midway airport, she officially becomes a young professional managing her own apartment, and she ceases to be my last dependent, domiciled on the shores of Lake Michigan.

We watch the spotted fawn scamper to the spot where its mother has planted herself, dead center in our neighbor's front yard. The pair is equidistant between our Ford and the black enamel front door of the rambling ranch-style home. The mother stands so still that she looks like a yard sculpture. Yet, her gaze at us is unwavering. Thick-lashed brown eyes scan our vehicle. When the passenger-side window makes its descent, her donkey-like ears telescope around.

The doe isn't as mature as other females that frequent the forested blocks south of our lake house. I decide either she is barely out of puberty or she struggled in the winter months to stay nourished due to her pregnancy. The deer population has reached epic size in many of the Northwest Indiana beach communities. Their numbers and inadequate food sources have pushed them into every domestic garden, yard, and driveway. There is talk of culling the herds due to the threat of disease from deer ticks and other vectors. That strategy, while healthier for the human population, would mean that this doe and fawn might not be relocated. Instead, she would be drugged, cornered, and hunted with arrows.

Now that the outdoors has seeped into the Ford Escort, my daughter's voice is a whisper. "Look. The baby is nursing on the mom." Whether it's nostalgia over my daughter leaving or this chance display of motherhood, tears dampen the frames of my sunglasses.

I drag my iPhone from my purse and zoom in. The fawn's little head bobs, tugging for milk at the mother's underbelly. Undeterred, the doe is locked in a stare-down with our windshield. She allows her famished offspring to take her fill while I click photographs. The thoughts in my head run the gamut: the doe is with her baby, and I'm with mine; she's taking care of her child as I do mine; that offspring is struggling to survive, while mine is starting a new way of life.

"This is so cool that we got to see this today. Right before I leave. That baby is my new favorite beach house memory," my daughter says.

I wipe away a tear that has found a path around my sunglasses. "Mine too," I say.

We are silent for a moment, and I pierce our contemplative mood. "I'll send you the picture, so you can post it to your timeline," I say.

In my head, I label it "Moment with Mother and Child," but the caption I send along with the photo to my daughter is "Nursing Fawn." The photo is one thing, but our shared experience is so much more.

BROKEN TRUST

When the house alarm emitted a series of short, shrill tones, I was immersed in meditation. I refocused on my mantra and tried to breathe deeply. A few seconds later, two more high-pitched beeps followed. I sighed and trudged over to the control panel. Haven't we all come to expect that electronics will let us down at some point? We love the conveniences of technology, but we know better than to trust them to operate at 100 percent efficacy forever.

And when it comes to people . . .

There are people we trust because they have proven we can count on them to treat us fairly, offer good advice, and keep our secrets. But there exist individuals who we expect more from but who let us down. These folks, the ones who disrespect or dishonor us, cause scar tissue to build up around our emotional center.

When I was in college, I shared a house with scores of my sorority sisters. At the end of the second-floor hallway was a huge walk-in closet where we stored fancy dresses and evening wear. When sorority rush came around, a traffic jam developed around the packed Formal Closet, and we had to take turns entering. Sometimes, the route from Formal Closet to our rooms resulted in trading formal wear with a friend to get something we fancied more.

Because I served on the Panhellenic side of the rush experience, I was not in my sorority house for Rush Week. Instead, I was sequestered in the Indiana University Memorial Union with fellow members of the Panhellenic Board and a lineup of sorority rush counselors. We wore sweatpants and sweatshirts, not fancy dresses, hose, and high heels. When Rush Week ended, I returned to my sorority house, where I met the new pledge class and learned in detail what had transpired during my absence by watching a slideshow. In one of the frames, I spied a roommate sporting the blue chiffon cocktail dress I'd stowed in Formal Closet.

The revelation was stunning. My roomie hadn't asked me if she could borrow the dress, and I wouldn't have let her if she had. It was my mother's dress, one that Mom had allowed me to bring to school with the promise I'd be careful with it. My sorority sister had overstepped the boundaries of our friendship, and as a result, our relationship fizzled. I reasoned if I couldn't trust her with my clothes, how could I trust her with my secrets? I forged other friendships.

No one was physically harmed in the borrowed dress example. It was just a dress and a thoughtless act by a casual friend. But what about those bigger trustbusters—the errors in judgment that, once discovered, don't just leave us scratching our heads but usher in disappointment, rejection, and loss?

In my first conversation with my birth mom, one of the first questions I asked was for my birth father's name. His identity had been legally omitted from my original birth record. I held my breath as she spelled out his last name. Armed with this information, my confidential intermediary launched a search for my father. Eighteen months later, my father still had not been found. The judge overseeing my search had no choice but to dismiss my case.

A year later, I hired a genealogist who stumbled upon my birth father's true identity. When I confronted my birth mother about this, she admitted she had given me the wrong information. Her lie caused me to distrust her. Our relationship stalled. Unlike the faulty house alarm panel and my college roommate, the bond with my birth mother was unique. Irreplaceable. Swapping her out for a new, improved model wasn't an option. Besides, I had spent a lifetime wondering about her and years trying to bring her into my life.

Someone wise said that trust takes years to build, seconds to destroy, and forever to repair. Faulty machines may be easier to fix than relationships, but from where I sit, the deep connections we forge with special people are worth the time and trouble.

WE ARE MEANING-MAKING
CREATURES

Afriend and I met for lunch at an outdoor café recently. Like most conversations these days, our chatter centered on the pandemic and our frustration with getting the vaccine. And as we always do, we shared updates about our twenty-something children and aging parents. Over Caesar salads and iced teas, we thought about the effect of isolation on our children's psyches, and about how the shutdowns impacted their work lives, living environments, and social lives.

We wondered what meaning our kids would draw from the "year like no other" and how it would impact their lives going forward.

During the pandemic year, my adoptive mother turned eighty-eight, a milestone to be sure. Mom spent nearly all of 2020 confined to her assisted-living apartment. For months, her only visitors were the nursing staff who appeared during the day to administer meds or drop off meal trays. My mother doesn't know how to turn on the old computer Dad used, nor is she interested in reading on an iPad or powering up the cell phone my sister bought for her. Electronically challenged, she depended entirely on her landline to communicate during the pandemic.

"Happy birthday," I sang into the phone. "How are you doing today?"

"Good, honey! Now that I've had my shots, I can go to the hair salon and mail room. I'm looking forward to celebrating tonight with my friends here in the dining room."

Mom's attitude is amazing but not surprising. Across the country, the elderly who have been spared the infection are crooning about life returning to normal. How did they make it through the hardships that COVID dished out? I don't have to quiz my mother about this; I can intuit her response.

In Mom's nearly nine full decades of life, she has dealt with many challenges: miscarriages and infertility, financial stress, the sudden death of a child and grandchild, and the loss of her spouse of sixty-four years. The challenge of the pandemic was a steep hill to climb, but one of many she has successfully traversed over a lifetime.

I think about my mother and my youngest daughter, who is single and in her twenties, and about all we have had to deal with because of the coronavirus pandemic. I wonder what meaning we can and will draw from the experience. For Mom, these months of isolation were another chapter in an incredible life. But I speculate whether my daughter will look back at this experience as the time she learned things it took her grandmother a lifetime to appreciate: the art of delayed gratification, the importance of resiliency and perseverance, and the acceptance of what one cannot control.

My mom has had a full life to gather her wisdom, but during the pandemic's isolation she would have benefitted from the merits of technology. My daughter weathered the lack of in-person socialization largely due to her electronic devices. Sixty years may separate my mother and daughter, but both have survived a binding historic event. I believe that the two have more in common now than was possible before the pandemic.

Wrapping up her birthday phone call, Mom said, "I'm looking forward to seeing you in person again."

Like my mother, I'm looking forward to the spring, too. I will have had my shots, so it will be safe to hug my loved ones again. The biggest takeaway from this bizarre year is the importance of optimism. Believing that better days were right around the corner got me through the tough spots.

WHO IS YOUR "I'LL BE RIGHT OVER" FRIEND?

I listen to a wide selection of radio stations when I drive. Car technology makes it easy to channel-surf and still focus on the road. Bored with the current news cycle and wanting a little country music buzzing in my veins, I landed on The Highway, a popular country radio station. As I cruised down the road on various errands, a question posed by the radio host hooked me.

The anchor asked, "Who is your 'I'll be right over' friend? Call in and share your stories."

I arrived at the grocery store before any callers were patched in, so I never got to hear their responses. Meandering through the produce aisles, I was so consumed by the call-in question that I nearly forgot the asparagus for dinner. Internally I quizzed myself: if I were to brave the radio-show vetting process, who would I claim as my "I'll be right over" friend? And which friend might say the same about me?

As I studied a heap of ripening avocadoes, I wondered if family members counted as friends for the purposes of the call-in question. I argued with myself: Friends are not family, but many of us might consider a certain family member as our IBROF.

My first inclination was to claim my identical twin as my IBROF. My twin sister has always been my first phone call when troubling news needs sharing. She heard about my breast biopsy results within minutes of the nurse informing me I had dense tissue, not cancer. One cold and snowy night when I was out of town and my husband wasn't answering his cell or our house phone, my twin sister drove to the house to check on him. She verified that his car was parked in the garage and that he hadn't slipped or conked out on our icy driveway. (He had in fact over-imbibed at a work dinner, left his cell phone in his coat pocket, and put himself to bed early!)

As I lingered in the long checkout lane behind an older couple who were complaining about the escalating prices of coffee and fancy waters, I decided I would not claim my twin as an IBROF simply because she's family. It's my experience that most people are able to count on family to go out of their way when the cry for help is issued. I wondered if I could come up with other candidates to claim as a "be right over" friend.

As I was running through a mental shortlist of dear friends, the cashier reminded me that I could remove my credit card from the card reader. Time to pay attention! I knew the dangers of pushing an unwieldy shopping cart through a grocery store parking lot on a Saturday afternoon. I sidelined all thoughts of the call-in question and focused on the journey to my car.

Just as my silver Tahoe came into sight, I heard a piercing scream two rows over. I craned my neck and saw a young mom coaxing a tired preschooler out of his car seat and into a hot shopping cart. He was trying to remove his bright blue T-shirt. The scene clicked a dusty memory into focus.

In August 1993, my family relocated to the Chicago suburbs. We were one week into a new house, schools, and neighborhood. My two daughters had started grammar school, but my four-year-old son's preschool program didn't start until after Labor Day. I had sliced open the tape on a moving carton and pulled out his Legos and matchbox cars, and then I left him to play quietly in his room while I unpacked boxes in the kitchen. A little later, I called up the back stairs to him. He didn't answer.

I scrambled up the stairs. A glance in my son's room informed me that he'd wandered off. My stomach clenched as I scoured the house. I checked all the bedrooms and bathrooms and peeked into the empty boxes crowding the detached garage. *Where had he gone?*

I shouted into the fenced-in yard and glared at the dog as if he could tell me where his little buddy had disappeared. Hands shaking, I combed through my purse for the names and numbers of two neighbors who'd welcomed me earlier in the week when our moving truck arrived. Both women promised to comb their yards and quiz their children.

I decided that before calling the police, I would take one more screaming pass through the disorganized house. A bright blue cloth in the upstairs bathroom caught my eye . . . was that my son's shirt? I followed a trail of clothes—khaki shorts, white socks, and black Velcro sneakers—which led to the door of my son's room. I bolted inside. A lock of mousy brown hair peeked out from under the comforter covering his bed. He was home! He must have been tired and climbed into bed for a nap. With tears in my eyes, I called my neighbors to share the good news and thank them for their help.

Tucked inside the Tahoe with my groceries in the back, I wondered if those two women, the neighbors in that story, would qualify as IBROFs. They had been willing to help me at a moment's notice. I cruised out of the grocery store parking lot, deciding not to call in to the radio show. But recently, I relived that memory with those very same women. Although they started out as strangers to me, over time they became my dear friends.

Sometimes when we need immediate help, the situation compels us to turn to people we don't know. All of us can recall times when strangers magically arose to meet an emergency, just as my neighbors did on that hot day in August 1993. Yes, those ladies were my IBROFs, even though I barely knew them. Almost three decades later, they are still the friends I'd call to come right over and lend a hand.

DIFFICULT QUESTIONS

One night at a teen sleepover, my friend and I, weary of the erratic darts and squiggles on the Ouija board, climbed into our sleeping bags.

She turned to me and asked, "You're adopted, right?"

Through my clenched jaw and prickly braces, two clipped words slipped out. "Uh . . . yeah." Then, like a boxer in the waning phase of his career, I waited for the sucker punch I knew would follow.

"What happened to your *real* parents?"

I can still feel the uncomfortable heat in my sleeping bag as I began to sweat. In response, I probably muttered something like *I dunno*, but inwardly I desperately wished that this question hadn't been posed. The shame of not knowing anything about my birth parents or my background festered until I located them in 2011 and 2014.

We have all fielded or launched them: difficult questions that leave the respondent feeling befuddled, angry, anxious, amused, or speechless. Queries like: Why do you think your marriage failed? How does it feel to be a widow? Don't you think you should watch your expenses at a time like this? Or even: Shouldn't you be wearing a mask?

If the environment is your workplace and it's your boss asking, then you have no choice but to offer some reply. When dealing with co-workers, friends, or the nosy woman across the hall, you have the option of politely declining to respond. Even so, experts agree that it's best not to dodge a difficult question completely. Instead, try to offer some sort of response that satisfies the questioner.

Here are three strategies I find helpful:

1. Ask for clarification. Clarifying the question before formulating an answer is an excellent strategy for confusing questions. My husband and I don't always use the same language, so this saves me from going off on the wrong tangent.

2. Buy time. When dealing with my aging mother, I take my time to respond, mostly because stalling helps me gather my patience. She tends to ask the same questions over and over.

3. Answer the parts you feel comfortable answering and ignore the rest. One friend of mine, when probed about something personal, is famous for responding, "What an interesting question!" or "You pose a really good question." Her words are part deferral and part buying time. She almost always skips any parts of the question she isn't comfortable responding to. This I deeply admire. Just because someone launches a query doesn't mean their question requires your attention.

I adopted these strategies later in life when I had to figure out how to handle the inevitable difficult questions adoptees face. My mom taught me many things, but it would have been great if, along with the birds-and-bees talk, she had given me a lesson on how to answer difficult questions about my adoption.

Here's the thing, though. When you know a question will keep coming your way, you perfect a response. That dopey response I offered at a teen sleepover—"I dunno"—morphed into other responses once I matured. For a while, I simply said, "It was a closed adoption. I have no information." Now, I'm fast to dish this out: "Do you have a few moments? Do you want the short or long version? I recently completed my adoption search, and I'm in reunion . . ."

So, why have I grown comfortable discussing my adoption? Because it allows me to talk about my memoir, my adoption blog, and other writing I'm working on. The knowledge I gained as I researched my adoption fills me with ease, and it erased the shame of all those years of not knowing.

Regarding handling other difficult questions, I still like my friend's approach best. "What an interesting question" buys you time to defer, decline, evade, and pick which part of a full response you wish to share.

FINDING INSPIRATION IN
AN UNLIKELY PLACE

For the better part of a week, I've had a problem with a key on my laptop. The letter *g* is stuck. Not just sticky, but frozen. Whenever it's depressed, no character appears. For a writer, a sticky key is annoying, a frozen key a nightmare. To make matters worse, the spell checker doesn't always kick in, so I've resorted to manually copying and pasting a *g* where it needs to be. Do you know how many words there are in the English language with the letter *g*?

When my *g* stopped performing, I struggled for about a half hour before nabbing a Genius Bar appointment at the Apple store. You know the drill. Five days out, the open slot I nabbed bumped hard into the dinner hour. Over the weekend, my *g* and I had frustrating writing sessions, so when the sun rose this morning, I did a happy dance. Finally, it was Monday: the day of unsticking my *g*.

I almost missed the longed-for Genius Bar appointment, and my fancy watch is partially to blame. In strapping it on this morning, I noticed it had gone the way of my sticky *g*. With just over an hour before I was due at the Apple store, I dashed into the jeweler to leave it for repair, knowing my cell phone would function as a timepiece in its absence.

During the trek across town from the jeweler to the mall, traffic built up behind a fender bender. As I checked the dashboard clock, I noticed the tire pressure warning light was on. (You can't make this stuff up.) The left front tire has been an intermittent issue, and I cursed the timing. The air kiosk at my friendly Mobil would have to wait. Fingers crossed I wasn't about to have a flat.

Loaded down with my computer backpack and wearing ballet flats, I hustled through the crowded mall parking lot, skirted around oblivious shoppers, and landed at Apple's threshold completely out of breath. With one minute to spare, I'd honored my time slot, but the technician didn't. I waited a whopping twenty minutes before he finally sauntered over. His face gleamed with appropriate Apple cheer as I explained my sticky *g* dilemma. With a nod and another smile, he disappeared into the back room with my computer.

Five minutes later, my laptop sported a new key, but this *g* was an identical twin to the old one—she was sticky, too. The ultimate solution was as appealing as being bumped from an oversold flight: mail in my computer for a keyboard overhaul, with an estimated turnaround time of seven days. If you're writing a monthly column, crafting a memoir, and taking an online course, being unplugged for twenty-four hours, much less seven days, is unthinkable.

"Don't you have a backup computer?" the Apple guy asked.

"Uh, yeah, except my ancient laptop isn't easily accessible." I glared at the familiar sight of a frozen *g* and sent ugly thoughts toward the ineffective and tardy Apple technician. I decided to forgo further service until my old computer was nestled in my hands.

So, I walked out of the Apple store in full possession of my laptop, no watch, and praying to all my favorite patron saints that, in my absence, the driver's-side front tire hadn't decided to kiss the pavement. Jumping back into rush hour traffic, I praised my trusty saints and called my favorite Mexican joint for takeout. Who tempts fate by cooking when the afternoon has already trembled with mechanical failures?

Since my takeout wasn't ready, I ventured into the restroom. The two regular stalls were occupied, but the handicapped one was free. I lucked into a stall the size of a small apartment. It was clean, it had plenty of hooks to hang up my purse and sweater, and it held not only a toilet bowl but also a full roll of toilet paper *and* a sink. It offered another bonus: a mural. "Hey Gorgeous" was stenciled in huge silver letters across the wall. I was chuckling out loud as I washed up. I exited the restroom, picked up my take-out order, and left a hefty tip with the hostess.

I don't make a habit of seeking inspiration in the ladies' restroom, but today's pick-me-up could not have been timelier. It's not every day you leave a public bathroom with a smile on your face, especially on the heels of an afternoon wrought with minor fiascos. With the scent of home-cooked Mexican tickling my taste buds and the memory of the bathroom mural perking up my mood, my grin survived the drive home. Focusing on the bathroom's cheeky compliment, I forgot all about the tire pressure warning light, the watch, and my frozen *g*. Those pesky problems will sort themselves out over time.

YOU NEVER KNOW

Writers are solitary creatures. We live in our heads, where we conjure scenes and characters to make our stories come alive, and we torture ourselves until we come up with the right string of words. Even more onerous than the revision process is the reality that, for our work to reach an audience, writers must submit for publication. And with publication comes the need for publicity. Writers love feedback, but we are more comfortable behind a computer screen than in the public eye. This has always been the case for me.

When I was a child, my mother and dad entertained regularly in our family's home. Every week it seemed that Mom was planning a dinner party for close friends, a neighborhood potluck, or a family picnic outing. As the oldest siblings, my twin sister and I were folded into Mom's party planning. The morning of the event, we scooped melon balls for a fruit salad or skewered appetizers and plated them according to my mother's specifications. In truth, I didn't mind these tasks. The creativity of the solitary tasks appealed to me, but I abhorred the stage that followed party prep.

As the party hour approached, my five siblings and I were sent to our rooms to clean up. Our parents expected us to make an appearance, mingle, and make small talk with their guests. During the ordeal, I longed to be upstairs in the room I shared with my sister, engrossed in a library book or finishing a homework assignment. Thrust into the limelight and compelled to offer polite replies to questions from my parents' dinner guests was well outside my comfort zone.

On May 11, 2021, two days after Mother's Day, my first book was released. *Twice a Daughter: A Search for Identity, Family, and Belonging* is the story of how my twin sister and I researched our closed adoption and connected with birth relatives. In advance of the book launch, my publicist arranged for a local paper in Sarasota to run an article about me and my book. When my husband tossed the *Longboat Observer* on the kitchen table, my breath caught. Spying my headshot in the headline banner, I became that shy, gangly teen who wished she was reading in her room instead of being showcased.

"Just put it over there," I said to my husband. "I'll look at it after I bring up the rest of the groceries from the car."

In the condo's lower-level parking area, I unloaded shopping bags from my car and placed them into one of the handy shopping carts the building provided for the owners. Several slots over from where I stood, one of the guys from the maintenance team hosed down a dusty sedan in the carwash bay. As I pushed my unwieldy shopping cart past him toward the elevator bank, the worker looked up and lifted his palm.

"Hey, Mrs. McGue," he said.

"Hi, Paul!" I returned the worker's smile and leaned over to straighten a bag tipping over in my cart.

Behind me, the sound of spraying water hushed, and then I heard hurried footsteps squeaking toward me. When I peeked up from the depths of the cart, Paul hovered pensively near my elbow.

"I saw the newspaper article, Mrs. McGue. I didn't know you were an author." Paul's callused hands held a damp towel.

As I thought about the newspaper I'd left on the kitchen counter, a familiar warmth crept into my cheeks. *Publicity, the necessary evil to reach target readers.* Inwardly, I sighed.

It was my turn to look shyly over at Paul. "Yes. I've been working on that book for almost ten years now."

"What is it about?" he quizzed.

I relaxed my hold on the shopping cart and turned to face Paul.

"My twin sister and I are adopted. When I was in my late forties, my health issues demanded that we look into our closed adoption. The book is about that process and the discoveries we made."

Paul's eyes widened and he twisted the towel in his hands. "My wife is adopted. We tried to find her biological family but no luck so far."

The way Paul looked off into the parking area, I had an inkling of how his heart ached for his wife's search disappointments. I stopped fussing with the items in the shopping cart. The groceries could wait. For ten minutes, Paul and I chatted by the elevator doors. Like me, Paul's wife was from a closed adoption and her adoptive parents had not been given any of her birth family's background or medical history. As I filled him in on all my efforts to find my birth parents, Paul's eyes never left mine.

"You're giving me hope, Mrs. McGue. Thanks." He turned and took a step toward the half-washed car.

"Hold on, Paul! I have copies of my book in the car. Let me get one for you. Perhaps something I tried will help put life into your wife's search."

I inscribed a copy of *Twice a Daughter* to Paul's wife and handed it over. He studied the cover, grinning ever so slightly.

Thanking me again, he tucked the book under his arm and walked back to the dirty car, whistling.

When I wheeled the grocery cart into our kitchen condo, I considered the newspaper lying on the counter. Holding it in my hands, I stared at the headline banner and my headshot, much as Paul had done with my book minutes before in the parking garage. The newspaper piece still elicited feelings of discomfort, but now I also felt heartened and gratified. Because of the article, I'd been led into a conversation with someone who needed hope.

As a writer, I doubt I will ever be comfortable with publicity and self-promotion. Given a choice, I would prefer to lounge in my room with a good book or to play with words on my computer. Yet, that is not how writers connect effectively with intended readers. In a small way I must credit my mom. By insisting my siblings and I venture into an uncomfortable setting, we learned the benefit of pushing beyond personal limitations. I realize that when we do this, we are gifted with the opportunity to make a difference.

SAVORING HOLIDAY CELEBRATIONS

I was in the yard re-claiming the dozens of tiny American flags I'd shoved into potted plants for the Fourth of July weekend. The recent rains had spackled them with garden soil and drenched them so thoroughly that the standards drooped precariously over the container rims. It seemed disrespectful to leave our nation's colors in such a state. So, I plucked the little flags, shook off the dried dirt, and set them on the front porch.

With only one week left in July, I figured it was time to dismantle the rest of the holiday decor and return it to storage. Next, I marched over to the star-spangled ribbons fastened to the fence gates. But on closer inspection, I reared back. Not because I favored the pair of oversized gaudy bows, but because a black spider the size of my thumb had covered the ribbons with her elaborate web. Perched atop the bow, she looked askance at me like a queen holding court. I'm not afraid of spiders, but squaring off with a worthy adversary was not on the day's to-do list.

I backtracked to the front of the house, where an expanse of large red, white, and blue buntings flapped and waved in the late-afternoon winds. I liked how they camouflaged the porch railings and whipped and twirled this way and that, as if they possessed a personality. I smiled, remembering all the years I'd hung those same buntings on other front porches in anticipation of one of my favorite holidays.

Then I wondered, "Do the decorations really need to come down before the calendar flips to August?"

I plopped down on the front stoop and reached for my water bottle. As I sat, enjoying my cold drink and the view of the yard, I recalled a similar decorating dilemma nearly one year ago. In July 2020, I trudged up to the storage area to collect the containers of Fourth of July decorations. As I heaved the first bin of party gear from the dusty shelves, I asked myself, "Why am I bothering to decorate at all?"

At that time, only four of us were in the house: my husband, my twenty-four-year-old daughter—she'd been working from our home since the lockdown went into effect—and my eighty-seven-year-old mother, whom we had sprung from her COVID-ridden senior living complex.

That year, July Fourth felt like the four of us were greeting another boring pandemic day instead of gearing up to celebrate our nation's birthday. Our tight little pod was not in a party mood, much less party mode. In fact, we weren't socially distancing. We were sequestered and shut off from all physical contact with extended family and trusted friends. By the Fourth of July, we had successfully avoided the virus. In staring at the party bin containing all the red, white, and blue paper products, it occurred to me that achieving this milestone was a cause for celebration.

So, I dragged all the holiday paraphernalia down the back stairs and into the kitchen. From the first bin I pulled out plates, trays, and napkins adorned with our nation's colors. Then I set the festive items around the dining table. Something about that effort had lifted my spirits—until I remembered that a home-cooked BBQ for our "Fab Four" was the only thing planned for the day.

All the local Fourth of July activities had been canceled. No fireworks—not even the haphazard homespun displays that usually light up the lakefront as far as the eye can see. Last year, the suspension of our annual community parade tugged at my heartstrings. The blocks-long stream of convertibles, mini-floats, and neighbors marching with their kids in decorated strollers and wagons is something the entire neighborhood anticipates. My kids had once ridden bikes and tricycles on which they'd attached patriotic streamers. Nostalgia and pangs of disappointment over all the canceled events almost forced me to return the decorations to the storage room.

Yet, I didn't. An inner voice had scolded me: July 4 is an important date. Don't let the pandemic erase celebrating it in some way.

So, I dragged the other storage bin outside to the patio. I strung the red-and-white-striped buntings with their blue fields of white stars along the porch railings. I snagged the ladder from the garage and draped the last bunting above the front door so our nation's colors could be seen far and wide. And just as I did this year, I stuffed tiny flags in the patio flowerpots, hung the big patriotic bows on the gate, and settled onto the top step of the front porch to sip a cold drink.

From this spot, I remembered how thrilled I'd been last year to see my neighbor from across the street out with his small kids. He'd yelled to me from the street below, "The place looks festive! Happy Fourth!"

I waved grandiosely and shouted back. "You, too!" That exchange alone pleased me and made me glad I'd gone to the effort to decorate.

Three hundred and sixty-five days later, a new and improved July Fourth finally arrived. My husband and I prepared our lake house for the arrival of our fully vaccinated guests: our adult children, their significant others, and extended family and friends. We packed the fridge with all the usual holiday party food like ribs and corn and coleslaw, and then we awaited the longed-for community parade and evening local fireworks displays.

From my perspective, this year's Fourth of July weekend was special, distinctive, and exceptional. Downright magical.

It felt grand to resume activities and events that I had always enjoyed but took for granted. Like hanging an overabundance of gaudy, patriotic decorations from every corner, railing, and post. Like inviting more guests to the family barbecue than I own chairs to accommodate. Like staying up way past the last snap, crackle, and big boom just to have one more drink with family and friends.

And we all did this, didn't we?

Because this year we could. And each of us needed the familiar, the expected, the usual Fourth of July celebrations. We craved it. And so, if some of us decide we want to leave up our Fourth of July decorations a little longer than might be deemed necessary, we shall. And we will feel good about it. Savoring holiday celebrations is good for our morale, important for maintaining our sense of community, and essential to the health and tenets of our nation.

WE SEE WHAT
WE WANT TO SEE

When my son was about a year old, I perched on the edge of a closed toilet and watched him grip the white rim of the porcelain bathtub. He squealed with delight each time I dropped a favorite bath toy under the running faucet. His pleasure with the colorful, bobbing plastic toys eased away the tiredness I felt from a day of mothering three children under the age of four.

With one eye on my precious little guy, I darted to the bathroom door and grabbed his hooded towel off the hook. In those few seconds—between glancing away from my toddler, nabbing the towel, and turning back again—I noticed something about my son that had escaped me until that moment.

As my little boy stood gazing into the tub, I saw that his right calf muscle was chunkier than the left one. Frozen at the bathroom door, I studied his body. The right leg was not simply more muscular. It was longer too. A sour taste crept into the back of my mouth.

No, how can this be? I wondered.

Next, I dropped to the floor and studied my little boy's legs from a different angle. As he giggled at the yellow duckie drifting below, I observed how his right knee bent slightly, naturally accommodating the difference in leg length.

How did I not notice this before?

After I chastised myself for being derelict in my parental responsibilities, I arrived at a conclusion. Neither of my two daughters had exhibited any kind of limb deformity, so I had not been looking for this in my third child. I had seen what I had wanted to see: another child developing normally. Yet, my head pounded with concern. How had the pediatrician missed the birth defect? What should my next steps be, and was this an indication of something else, a more serious underlying health matter?

Several days ago, I opened an email from a reputable literary firm that reviews writers' published work. Months ago, I submitted my manuscript for critique, a critical step toward gaining recognition and coaxing more readers to pick up my memoir, *Twice a Daughter.*

When I opened the attached critique, I thought, *No, how can this be?*

The paid reviewer awarded my book three stars out of five, a much lower ranking than reviews I'd garnered elsewhere. My stomach tightened.

I scanned the analysis, wondering what it was about my new book that the reviewer found less compelling than other critics. Was it my writing style—my bent toward crafting memoir that reads like fiction versus a more literary narrative—or was it my characterizations or dialogue that had not rung true enough in her estimation? I knew that stories of overcoming adversity were becoming more commonplace. Perhaps my book had been lumped by the reviewer into that crowded category.

I read the review again.

Besides a few factual errors (my sister's name was spelled wrong), a phrase caught my eye. The reviewer labeled my five-year search for birth relatives—one incited by a breast biopsy—as an "ongoing middle-class, middle-American experience."

I bristled.

Nowhere in my manuscript had I used the words *middle class* to describe my story. My memoir is about navigating the closed-adoption experience and reconnecting with birth relatives. In my head, I argued with the reviewer: Adoption is an experience that transcends class, ethnicity, and geography. Adoption is universal; its prevalence covers the globe. Yet somehow the reviewer had made assumptions from the words that I wrote, and she had focused on those suppositions when crafting her evaluation.

Much like the day I noticed my son's birth defect, once I got over the shock of the review, I speculated whether another issue was at play. Before dismissing the review, I scrutinized my manuscript. I hail from the Midwest and grew up in a middle-class family. But in crafting my story, I had not meant for the reader to latch onto those facts. My intention was to emphasize my struggle to find identity, family, and belonging, things that I was deprived of due to my closed adoption.

I was puzzled by the situation.

Perhaps the reviewer saw my book as another middle-class adult woman writing about her troubles. Admittedly, on a basic level, the book contains those elements. But why highlight demographics and ignore the book's meatier themes of rejection, loss, acceptance, and forgiveness?

And so, I wonder.

Is our first inclination to see only what we want to see? Is it only by chance that we put on the proverbial other set of glasses, lenses that shift our gaze from a more mundane perspective to the veiled place where profound truths reside?

The day after the bathtub scene, I whisked my son off to the pediatrician. Until he became a teenager, he underwent annual examinations with numerous specialists. To this day he has not manifested any of the potentially serious effects of an onerous diagnosis, and the larger, longer leg has not prevented him from leading an active life. But I gleaned something valuable from that chapter in my life. I have become a careful, vigilant observer who questions the obvious.

While I'd like to ask the reviewer to re-read my book with the hope that fresh insights might emerge for her, that isn't an option. The parameters of the review process are such that the writer must choose to accept the review—forever linking its publication with the manuscript—or kill it. Ultimately, I chose the latter because I felt that the review did not adequately cover my work.

And, if I could communicate with the critic, I would offer this counsel: Take the time to analyze further than is your inclination; truths screaming to be championed lurk below every surface. Diving deep is what we do when we care.

TOLERATIONS

One Monday at 5:00 a.m., my condo building's fire alarm blared. The undulating screeches—which continued for a solid thirty minutes—alternated with a woman's kind but insistent voice informing my husband and me: *There has been a fire reported in your building. Please leave your unit and find safety. The fire department is on its way.*

To my husband, I muttered, "What next?" and to myself, *How much more can I tolerate?*

This past year while we watched the nation battle the pervasive pandemic, the surges of racial unrest, and a contested, divisive presidential election, I was embroiled in my little world of misery. In October, the week that my husband and I were to leave our home in northwest Indiana to spend the winter in Sarasota, we got a midnight phone call: our upstairs neighbor's water heater had flooded our newly decorated condo. This dumb luck affected several other units and the condo lobby, too.

Misery does love company.

For weeks, my husband and I fought to get an insurance adjuster to come out and evaluate the waterlogged insulation and drywall, wrecked carpets, and tile floors and to give us an allowance for repairs. Concurrent with the drama of gathering our items and putting salvageable furnishings into permanent storage, we interviewed quality contractors who could restore our unit to its previous condition.

During these nerve-wracking weeks, we scrounged for suitable interim housing, a rare commodity given that the "snowbirds" had booked the best rentals the previous year. The skinny is that a nearby, fully furnished rental with beach access magically opened up. The owners had intended to replace all the windows and doors but due to COVID-related manufacturing and shipping delays, the unit was immediately available. We considered ourselves lucky . . . until a tropical storm/Category 1 hurricane came bounding in. As my husband and I hid in the bathroom, away from the rattling and needing-to-be-replaced doors and windows, I was reminded of my youth. In the Midwest, my siblings and I grabbed our flashlights and scrambled to the basement, waiting for the tornado sirens to go off. Yet, in this tiny Florida condo, there was no basement, and the flashlight we found in the back of the silverware drawer lacked batteries. I scolded myself. As a past Girl Scout leader, hadn't I been trained to be better prepared?

Of course, nothing could have prepared me for all the annoying mishaps that transpired after the hurricane galloped on. A closet organizer collapsed, strewing our few belongings this way and that. Next, one of the closet doors separated from its frame, and I got a nasty sliver trying to push it back together. Sweet ants marched in through cracks and crevices, assuming complete ownership of the first-floor unit.

The ultimate insult was that the ants repeatedly infested the filter in the gourmet coffee maker, which I had lugged over from our water-deluged condo. I'm proud to be part of the generation that grew up with the jingle: "The best part of wakin' up is Folgers in your cup." A true "I need my coffee to start the day" kind of person, the ants' repeat appearances in the coffee maker traumatized me.

There is always more to endure if we look for it.

As I write this, the master bath sink is slow to drain, black mold clings to the caulk in the shower, and the fridge has decided to freeze everything on the two bottom shelves. I also doubt that the dishwasher can sanitize the hodge-podge of dishes I shove in there.

Enough already. Here's the good news.

Our old condo has been restored and will soon be ready for us to move in. My husband got both Covid shots, and I'm scheduled for my first one at home in Indiana. Our nation survived the "year like no other," and the president has promised that everyone will be eligible to receive the vaccine by May 2021. Life may return to the old normal around July 4.

After surviving the pandemic year with most of my sanity intact, I have a new outlook on toleration. When we are subjected to more challenges than we think we can cope with, we find a way to endure. We can all tolerate more than we expect. Thanks to humor, sunshine, exercise, and the willing ear of a sister, neighbor, or golf partner.

MY WRITING SPACE KEEPS SHRINKING

A few years ago, my husband and I sold our old Victorian in Chicago's western suburbs where we raised our four children. We left Illinois for northwest Indiana and moved into a home perched on a sand dune overlooking Lake Michigan. The downsizing, geographical switch, and change of pace were liberating. It's also been the perfect recipe for taking my writing to a different level—from a hobby to a later-in-life second career.

For a dedicated writing space in our new home, I claimed a small room at the top of the stairs. I painted it a bluish-green reminiscent of a Tiffany shopping bag. Above a new, sleek glass desk, I hung a favorite acrylic showcasing an Impressionistic spring garden. From an ergonomically designed desk chair, I glean inspiration from the painting, feed an insatiable Epson a diet of clean white paper, and peruse files and resources from the adjacent stack of crammed bookshelves.

The setup is efficient, intimate, and idyllic, but the best part of my office is the wall of windows. The bank of glass allows me to soak in the sun as it glides across the southern sky. When I write in this niche, it's almost as if I'm working outdoors. And so, my struggles with theme, word choice, and grammar feel less like a battle and more like a stolen pleasure. From this loft in the clouds, I launched my author website, penned my first blogs, and pitched my local paper for a monthly byline.

Life can be lovely. It's also dynamic.

On Christmas Day in 2017, our married daughter living in Sarasota announced that she was expecting our first grandchild. The notion of escaping the dreary and cold midwestern winters to spend more time with our growing family in the Sunshine State was a clear-cut decision. Like most snowbirds, we landed in a nice condo. A building with a gulf view and full amenities trumped space concerns.

For a long-time married couple used to spreading out at opposite ends of a single-family residence, the two-bedroom condominium layout begged compromise. My husband nabbed the desk area in the family room, and I ordered a small writing desk for a corner in the master bedroom. To the sounds of the ocean's surf, I tinkered on my laptop while the southern sun warmed my shoulders.

Whenever I needed a fresh idea or new perspective, I rode the elevator to the lobby and commandeered the cushy common-area room overlooking the entry gardens. I nicknamed this seldom-used space *my other office*; it's even equipped with its own bathroom. While the circumstances are not quite as ideal as my writing lair on the shores of Lake Michigan, it's been beneficial. Over the two years we lived in that apartment, I added weekly blogs to my website and began crafting my memoir about the search for my birth relatives.

Whenever life hits a high note, expect a downbeat.

When the pandemic shut down the world in March 2020, condo management deemed all the public spaces in our building off-limits—the door to *my other office* would be locked for the foreseeable future. Thus confined, I roamed the limited square footage of our apartment armed with my laptop. When the sun came up, I was ensconced in a nook in the kitchen, editing my memoir. After a lengthy, masked-up morning walk, I shuffled between the bedroom's small writing desk, a recliner in the den, and a lounge chair on the balcony. Fueled by the coastal sun as a constant and the peripheral ocean view, I scribbled in notebooks or tapped into my laptop. I blogged. I slogged through the final chapters of my memoir. And I counted the days until spring was in full bloom up north so I could return to my perfect little writing room on the Great Lakes.

The shutdown inserted more family into our household.

Six weeks before our planned return to Indiana, our son and his girlfriend learned that the remainder of their final term at Notre Dame would be entirely virtual. They abandoned the dense university environment for the safety of our home on Lake Michigan. Two weeks after that, my youngest daughter's DC office shut down. Faced with working from home in a city high-rise apartment, elbow-to-elbow with a roommate, she chose to join her brother and ride out the lockdown at the lake house.

When we arrived from Florida in early May, my son had spread out in my husband's office and my daughter had made my office her own. Despite my publishing deadlines, I didn't have the heart to kick her out. So, I invoked the routine I'd established in Florida. At sunrise, I wrote at the kitchen counter, shifted with the morning light to a game table in the family room, and then at mid-day when the sun was high in the sky, I lifted the bedroom shades and plopped into a comfy chair with my laptop. Before the heat and humidity of the midwestern summer set in, I submitted my completed memoir to my publisher.

A year like no other continues its barrage of inconveniences.

Three days before our annual return to the Sarasota condo, a circulating valve failed on the water heater in the apartment directly above ours. In the dead of night, water streamed into the walls and floors of every unit from the sixth floor down to the lobby. When we arrived to assess the damage, it was clear our *home away from home* would be uninhabitable for months. While water experts set up commercial fans and ripped out drywall, movers arrived to haul our furnishings and belongings off to storage. Amidst arguments with the insurance company over the timing and scope of the renovation, we hunted for long-term housing.

With "the season" about to commence, finding a place to live was daunting. The stress of the situation shut my writer's brain down for two full weeks. By a strange stroke of luck, a roomy rental with beach access suddenly became available. Designed with furnishings for vacation living, the unit lacked desk areas and comfy chairs. But the wall of windows opening out to a small balcony faced south. Natural light with outdoor space—we signed the lease! A week later, we wedged a desk from our condo into the back bedroom for my husband, and I spread out my computer and notebooks at one end of the knotty pine kitchen table. Within days, I was back to blogging and submitting essays on schedule.

I've gotten used to the stiff kitchen chair, Hobby Lobby artwork, and skimpy storage in our temporary quarters. The setup is not ideal: I'm not connected to a printer; I'm not surrounded by my favorite books and resources; the room is not painted my favorite blue; the common areas are not accessible due to the pandemic's resurgence. Yet, I'm still honing my authorial voice. In fact, I'm putting out the same amount of content as I did last spring while sheltering in place and when I returned to the cozy lake house writing spaces.

I've come to believe productive writing is less about the quality of the workspace or the size of the writing desk. It's more about the cultivation of a consistent writing habit regardless of circumstances. For me, a set routine, unobstructed daylight, and access to the outdoors have been the keys to perpetuating my hobby-turned-career.

DOES ANYONE HAVE
A CELL PHONE CHARGER?

Remember what everyday life was like before we heard of a place in China called Wuhan? Costco had plenty of paper goods. The airports bustled. When traveling, our worst fear was a weather delay on flights we'd overpaid for months earlier. Few of us obsessed over hand sanitizer and latex gloves. Most of us looked askance, not enviously, at the stray individual wearing a face mask. It's a time for which we all long for a speedy return.

Five months ago, the term COVID-19 had not yet been coined. It was mid-December, and the big news story was New Year's Eve and the sparkling new decade ahead. The frenetic pace of the holidays presented us with different struggles than we have now. After spending the afternoon preparing appetizers or running to the mall for a last-minute gift, we greeted guests with a mug of eggnog or a flute of champagne. Those of us in airports over the holidays had gifts in our suitcases, ones we hadn't worried about wiping down or spraying with Lysol.

Given the current crises, I laugh at myself as I pen these next words. Outside of feeding and gifting my family, my biggest dilemma at Christmastime was keeping my spouse and adult children from snatching my cell phone chargers.

For the last fifteen years, my immediate family has traveled to Montana in December. Big Sky is a remote destination. There are a few mom-and-pop groceries, a handful of decent restaurants, and a hardware store, but you won't find a dry cleaner or a car wash. So, every year when we head out West, I overpack. Besides extra socks and thermal underwear, I layer my bag with gadgets galore: scissors, tape, hooks for the Christmas tree, treasured ornaments so the tree looks homey, wine openers, a small sewing kit, and packets of foot warmers. My family counts on me for that miscellany. This year, I realized my tendency to over-prepare only enabled my family's forgetfulness.

When we arrived at the log home, I plugged my iPad into one of my chargers in the bedroom. The second one I brought to the kitchen with my phone. During our first night cooking, I watched my daughter unplug my phone and move both to an outlet by the sofa. When we turned on Netflix, the long white cord, which I had responsibly toted from Chicago, was plugged into her cell phone, not mine. "I forgot mine," she said with a sweet smile. I responded, "I guess we can share." When the movie was over, I carried my cell phone to the bedroom. There, I discovered my iPad was untethered and in its place was my husband's cell phone.

The second day of vacation began with the same steal-mom's-chargers routine. The charger-swapping mess obliterated the spirit of Christmas. All of us being addicted to our devices wasn't the issue. The mountains are prone to hostile weather, and my kids are adventurous skiers. For my family's safety, we needed accessible, well-charged phones. To purchase USB cords locally would have meant a three-hour round-trip drive on a two-lane canyon road.

Online ordering was the obvious solution. We struggled for a few days, but eventually I equipped the log home with several docking stations and enough USB cords to charge a football team. The ease with which we got up and running became integral to the success of our family vacation. Connectivity and a reliable supply chain were the answer to our family's holiday dilemma. Those two factors play a significant role now as the country addresses uncertainty.

I wish our nation had been in a better place to deal with this pandemic. What we lack regarding medical supplies and preparedness is more serious than not having enough cell phone chargers. It's easy to regret what one doesn't have. Yet, we have no other option than to make do. I don't believe we're ever as ready as a situation requires. It may be as simple as this: We cannot expect to be adequately prepared if we are blind to the choices of others.

THE CENTER OF THE
CINNAMON ROLL

When the news broke that the Delta variant was chiseling away at the efficacy of each COVID-19 vaccine and we would soon need a booster, I stared at the TV newscaster. I puzzled how this could be happening so soon after normal activities had resumed.

And as I listened to wave after wave of news shows validate the startling findings, I squirmed. Thoughts of a redo—resuming the worn-out pandemic routine of uncomfortable masks, social-distancing, isolation and virtual contact—didn't just usher in disappointment. I found the news deflating. It was as if someone had pierced all the party balloons and banned fun forever.

Several years ago, before federal laws mandated all travelers don face masks for air travel, my husband and I were switching planes in the Minneapolis airport with our four kids. Because we had flown out of the Chicago area at dawn, breakfast options were slim to nonexistent. My husband handed the kids each some money. "Grab some breakfast. Hurry back. Our next flight boards soon."

Our oldest daughter, who was a teenager at the time, trotted off with her youngest sister in tow in search of a greasy breakfast sandwich. The two middle kids followed the sugary scent of hot cinnamon rolls down the moving walkway. My husband and I huddled at the connecting gate, enjoying a quiet cup of hot coffee. I was less concerned about my rumbling gut as about the four of them returning in time to make the next flight.

My "bookend" daughters returned first and nestled into seats beside me. The eldest handed my husband a hot egg and cheese sandwich. I peeked at my watch, then at the airline attendant. She studied a computer console and held a microphone in one hand as if an announcement was imminent. With our ten- and twelve-year-olds nowhere in sight, I stood and craned my neck in each direction. My heart took off in a gallop. I knew if we missed our flight, there wasn't another one until later that night. To my husband, I muttered, "I'm going to look for the kids."

The words no sooner formed than the tardy pair emerged from the throng of passengers flooding an adjacent gate.

"You were gone a long time," I scolded.

The twosome ignored me and plopped down by my husband. When they opened the white Styrofoam containers, an aroma of toasted bread and sugary sweetness filled our area. If the airline attendant hadn't chosen that moment to issue the first boarding call, I would have closed my eyes and savored the scent of warm cinnamon.

Instead, I said, "Hurry up. Eat."

My words were rewarded with frowns and eyerolls. From experience, I knew my children consider eating a cinnamon roll a serious endeavor. It is an act of reverence. First, they devour the crispy, brown edges of the bun, then they work their way to the gooey middle drenched in cinnamon and warm vanilla frosting. Saved for last, the delectable center usually is devoured in one big bite.

I rose from my seat, strapped on my backpack, and pulled our boarding passes from my purse. My husband nodded at me, then considered the kids' poky efforts with their cinnamon rolls. I don't know if he meant to speed up their breakfast or if the sight of the bun's savory center was too much to take. He grabbed a fork, leaned over, and snagged the prized middle from my son's breakfast bun.

The entire family gasped.

The expression on my son's face was one for the record books. His stricken look contrasted with my husband's smacking lips. All this confusion was set to the background refrain of the airline attendant proclaiming, "Boarding all rows, now, for the flight to Bozeman."

Before I could chastise my husband for snatching food from a child's mouth, he gave my son a stern look: "Get over it, son. It's time to board the plane. There are more cinnamon rolls in your future."

As I think of this family anecdote and juxtapose it against the latest pandemic wrinkle, this recent setback is not unlike having the center of the cinnamon roll stolen away. The initial shock is maddening. The loss is deflating. Regrouping is a given.

Indeed, there are more cinnamon rolls to be had. Normalcy will return. It's just a matter of when. Reaching that milestone entails stretching our patience once again. I suppose one bonus is that we are better at delaying gratification than ever before.

There is plenty to be concerned about, but a tiny, new worry is niggling in the corner of my mind. I hope the cinnamon roll franchise will not be another business that meets its demise due to COVID.

HOW LONG BEFORE WE SET ASIDE OUR COVID-TINTED GLASSES?

Like you, I watched with horror as the coronavirus besieged China, Italy, Europe, and New York, then silently invaded the remaining US states. Sheltering in place and gearing up to venture out became irksome protocols to fend off the unwelcome international visitor. Within weeks of toasting a new decade, we were thrust into a global pandemic. Now, everything we do, watch, read, and think about is tainted by the virus.

In mid-May, my husband and I returned from our winter getaway in Sarasota to our home on Indiana's lakefront. This coincided with the state's reopening from the lockdown. As we pulled into our driveway, the tense muscles in our legs and backs eased, but the Lysol wipes and paper masks on the console reminded us of what we hadn't left behind. While Lake Michigan's cool breezes promised a reprieve from the lung-tightening heat and draining humidity of Florida, our journey home meant more self-quarantining. Nonetheless, being home felt delicious, and I was eager to slip into familiar routines.

This morning, I took my first cup of coffee out to the side porch, plopped into one of the wicker rockers, and waited for the sun to peek through the neighbor's forsythia hedge. The dune grass did little to conceal me and my nubby gray bathrobe from the two-lane county road below, but I couldn't have cared less. With my feet folded under me, I gripped my coffee mug and set the dusty rocker into a gentle glide. Steam rose off the scalding brew, fogging up my glasses. I slid them over my nose into a makeshift headband, closed my eyes, and savored the lakeshore scents that drifted up to me.

Eyewear absent, I pressed my lips to the coffee mug and dared a sip. (What is it about one hampered sense that intensifies the other four?) As the scalding java wafted hints of dark chocolate under my nose, I noticed two large crows circling overhead, cackling like grandmothers. When a flock of robins added to the cacophony with their maniacal chirping, I stopped the rocker, unfolded my legs, and grabbed my glasses.

Something had set nature on edge.

I scanned the ridgeline of the dune. Nothing. As I zeroed in on the roads below, something in my periphery moved. Whipping my head around, I felt my breath hitch in my chest. Two feet away from my rocker, masked eyes studied me. Unperturbed by my seated presence, the critter crept closer to the nearby barbecue grill.

I clapped my hands together with such vehemence that both palms stung like a bug bite. Pounding my feet on the bluestone patio, I hissed an order. "Get outta here!" The raccoon tossed me an annoyed look, squeezed through the porch railing, and sauntered across the road. It stopped on the other side, cocked its head in my direction as if to check that I was watching its retreat, and then vanished into the forsythia.

I have a long and turbulent history with raccoons, and with each encounter my disdain has escalated. Picture books portray them as cute, cuddly animals. They are anything but. They're dangerous, disease-riddled pests. Unwelcome, just like the virus.

Thirty years ago, I left my two daughters, ages four and two, playing with their toys on our screened-in porch. I'd gone to the kitchen for something, and when I returned there was a raccoon on the other side of the screen door watching the girls play. Freaked out, I chased the scoundrel off and vowed never to leave my children alone on the porch.

Just as epidemiologists have warned us to expect a second wave of the virus, back then naturalists warned me that my nemesis, the raccoon, would show up again. Early one evening as I pulled into my driveway, I witnessed a raccoon scaling the garage gable. Nimbly, he breached the cupola and disappeared into the second-floor storage area.

Yikes! Not only had the creature broken into our home, but it had also been using our storage area as a toilet room. Wildlife experts were called in to capture and relocate the furry hoodlum, and then a clean-up crew bedecked in hazmat gear spent days disinfecting the space. Sealing up the cupola with metal screening was the final insulting expense.

This morning as I fixated on the forsythia hedge and tightened the belt on my robe, I knew the creature's return was inevitable. I left my coffee to grow cold and scanned the patio for weaponry. I retrieved a gnarly piece of driftwood from under an end table and snatched a handful of hefty rocks, remnants from a beach walk.

When the raccoon reemerged, I was ready. Aiming carefully, I whipped the rocks (my grown son, with whom I played countless games of catch during his little league years, would have been proud of my aim). The torrent of rocks scared off the persistent scoundrel, and I never had to swing the driftwood.

As I reflect upon this nerve-racking morning adventure, I can't help but compare this brief battle with the one we wage as a nation against the coronavirus. To defend ourselves against the virus, we grasp as I did for every available weapon: PPE, social distancing, sanitizer, remdesivir, steroids, plasma, ventilators, and vaccine research. Undoubtedly some of them, perhaps all of them will help vanquish COVID-19.

And, as I consider my insignificant experience with the raccoon, I'm left wondering: How long will it take before we stop evaluating everything that happens to us through the lens of the coronavirus?

THE POWER IN KNOWING

It's late on a Saturday afternoon, and I'm finally taking ownership of my favorite wicker lounge chair in the sunroom. I've been looking forward to this moment all day. Sufficiently wilted from transitioning the summer garden into fall, I'm equally weary of writing deadlines, submissions, and emails. I settle into the chair's floral cushions and let my gaze drift over the steep ridge of dune grass to Lake Michigan's shoreline. Something about the steady rolling pattern of the waves eases my weariness. It feels good to get out of my head and be soothed by the vast landscape.

When Hobbes, my son's mini-Australian shepherd, scampers in and hops up onto the adjacent lounge chair, I don't shoo him off the furniture. I understand Hobbes' intention. We both appreciate a good vantage point and the ability to see beyond the usual restrictions. We find power in knowing what is beyond the immediate.

Since my memoir came out in May 2021, one of the questions I'm often asked is: How has your life changed now that your book has made it into readers' hands?

The simplest answer is I enjoy connecting with my readers. It's an honor and a privilege to receive and respond to readers' questions and comments. Hearing how my story impacts my target audience is something I take seriously, and it is influential in crafting my next book.

When a writer crafts a story, usually only a handful of people have experienced it as it took shape. Often this includes a spouse, a teacher, peers in a writing course, a critique group, an editor, or a reviewer. Even having received feedback from those discerning folks, an author has no idea how the broader world will respond. When readers take the time to reach out with feedback, it's deeply gratifying to the author. Immersed in this stage of the writer's journey, I find it heart-warming and validating.

There is another layer, a deeper thread, to this question of how my life has changed since my book came out. And it has little to do with book publishing.

Life was immediately altered for me when I launched my adoption search in 2010. It was transformed again when I located and connected with various birth relatives. Subsequently, the act of writing about this period of my life served to deepen my awareness, and it afforded me healing and growth. Essentially, by seeking out my background and family history, I found pieces of myself I hadn't realized I lacked. As a result of completing my adoption search and crafting a memoir, I discovered my voice and a sense of purpose.

Much like Hobbes—who shifts this way and that in his wicker chair so he can study the beach beyond and the traffic below—I'm satisfied where I have landed. Daily life had been satisfying before I researched and published a book, but now the landscape of my life is broader, livelier, and richer. Sometimes we cannot know what is possible unless we challenge ourselves, shift our view, and consider new perspectives with an open mind.

WHAT TO SAY TO RIDICULOUS PEOPLE IN UNBEARABLE SITUATIONS

When my husband and I were raising our four kids—whose ages spanned a decade—dealing with their various developmental stages meant shifting gears on a dime. One kid would be on the downhill slope of puberty's emotional roller coaster while another one was dealing with plain old thirst or hunger. Family life was an exercise in triage: deal with the most unhappy person first, and then go down the list.

On one of those weekends when my husband and I agreed to divide and conquer—e.g., he had two kids to tote to Saturday AYSO soccer while I had the baby with me at our eldest's hotter-than-heck indoor swim meet—he coined a phrase that, today, still gets the family giggles going.

After soccer game number one, my hubby hustled the "middle" kids into the car. He was in a race to cross town to the next kid's soccer game. Sweaty soccer star number one squealed and whined. The tantrum no doubt had something to do with missing out on the sugary treats being handed out equally to winners and losers. My husband scooped up the malcontent, plopped him into the backseat, and clicked the seatbelt. This manhandling only intensified our entitled little athlete's histrionics.

My husband snapped, "You can't always get what you want. Get over yourself."

"Get over yourself!" *Isn't that a beaut?* This phrase has become my favorite comeback when dealing with ridiculous people in unbearable situations.

One week into 2022, just as the Omicron variant showed signs of slowing down, I slouched, bleary-eyed, in a hospital waiting room while my husband underwent surgery for cancer. I glanced up as a couple entered the small area and checked in with the staff member at the desk. When a nurse led the husband off for surgery, the wife took a seat close to me and the electronic patient progress board.

But she didn't settle into the cushioned vinyl seat. Seconds after sitting, she stood. She paced. And then she strutted back up to the desk.

In a clear voice, she said, "We were scheduled for the first surgery slot but got bumped. My husband's procedure was set up three weeks ago."

To which the desk attendant said something like, "The surgery schedule often changes."

I heard all this while rummaging in my purse for a nail file.

The woman wandered back to where she'd left her things. Standing, she surveyed the room. When I peeked up at the surgery board, her eyes whipped to mine.

"Is your husband here for surgery?" she asked.

Thinking she was looking for a friend with whom to commiserate, I answered quickly, "Yes, he is."

She leaned toward me. "What time is his surgery?"

In retrospect, I suppose that if I'd had enough coffee in me, I might have realized where the conversation was headed.

"It started at 7:00 a.m.," I said, squinting up at her.

"Who's the doctor?" she persisted.

My brain was still resting on a warm pillow at home, so even though her query blew several HIPAA bells and whistles, I supplied the surgeon's name.

"Ah-ha," she proclaimed, puffing herself up like a proud detective who'd just unearthed the final clue to a tricky crime case. "You took our spot."

You took our spot?

My voice stalled at the back of my throat while my brain screamed curses like "you are just a nosy busybody, a troublemaker, and a HIPAA violator."

Eventually, my tongue scooped up more appropriate words. "I'm sure the surgeon had his reasons for changing the schedule."

And then I dished her a benign smile and turned my head away.

I dismissed her. Not because I wanted to be rude. Not because of her insensitive breach of my family's privacy. But for the sole reason that I was stifling an evil chuckle.

You see, what had suddenly popped into my head were the words: *Get over yourself!*

THE HAPPIEST MOMENT

My friend and I sprawl out at a prime terrace table at our favorite lunch spot. We order iced teas and agree to split the harvest salad and the best chicken quesadillas on the planet. After we've caught up on the recent happenings in our busy lives, my friend poses a startling question:

"What would you say was the happiest moment of your life?"

Before answering, I savor the last bite of my crispy quesadilla wedge, one I had infused with just the right smear of guacamole. This kind of penetrating query is one I often field from Robbie, and it's one of the reasons I enjoy our frequent lunch dates.

I met Robbie four years ago on the tennis courts. Before COVID struck, Robbie lost her husband to a prolonged battle with cancer. She spent the better part of the COVID year sequestered and alone, coping with debilitating grief and loss. Robbie has shared with me how she misses her husband's easy laugh, doting presence, and it-can-wait-'til-tomorrow attitude. She admits to craving the return of a life like the one they led during their decades of happy marriage. Sometimes during our gabfests, she laments how easily a widow is sidelined when couples formulate their weekend plans.

I wipe my gooey fingers on the linen napkin in my lap and study Robbie. The way her dark eyebrows arch to meet the brim of her straw fedora, I know she means for me to carefully consider her startling question. I assume she has been reflecting upon the happiest moments in her life, and I suspect I'm not the first or last friend she will poll with this thought-provoking query.

I drain my iced tea and ask for clarification, "The happiest moment. Just one moment? Not a time in my life?" I wish I could see the expression lurking behind her mirrored sunglasses.

Robbie's auburn hair flutters around her face in the light afternoon breeze. At seventy-two, she could easily pass for sixty. She grins. "Yep. The happiest moment. Pick one!"

She settles into the blue canvas seat cushions of her rattan lounger, pleased with herself for steering our lunch conversation into a positive and interesting lane. My brain pulses. Happy moments burst forth like heated popcorn kernels. Each joyful moment from my sixty-two-year existence vies for the lead.

"Okay," I say and scoot my chair closer to Robbie's. "I could claim the day I got married was my happiest moment. Or the days my children were born. Or the day my book was published. But I won't. While those events were each momentous and important, I expected to be happy . . ."

Robbie nods so energetically that her straw hat slips off the back of her head. "Go on," she says, retrieving it from under the table.

As I struggle to settle on a favorite "happiest moment," I contort the linen napkin in my lap. "While those moments I just mentioned were happy, they were also stressful. So, I guess what I mean is my happiness during those times included, well . . . relief! Relief that everything turned out as I'd hoped." I giggled. "Steve didn't leave me at the altar, childbirth was not too difficult, and the kids came out with all their fingers and toes."

Robbie takes off her sunglasses. Her impish grin crinkles her blue-green eyes. "Keep going," she pleads. "I can tell by the way your eyes shone a moment ago that there's something else you want to offer as your final answer."

Feeling a little like a guest on *Jeopardy*, I giggle again. She's right. There was another thought jockeying for position. I'd initially ignored it, mostly because the other "happiest moments" felt more appropriate, like they were what I thought I should say.

"Okay . . ." I draw out the syllables to buy time.

My brain pounces on the shy memory and pushes it forward. Under this intense focus, it sparkles and gleams like a diamond catching the light just right. This particular "happiest moment" had been a yearned-for success. One that was a lifetime in the making. Being granted this wish made me so deliriously happy, completed me in such a way that, when it came to fruition, I think my heart stopped for a second.

Just as I'm about to speak, the waitress appears with a pitcher of tea. As Robbie and I watch her fill our glasses, I rack my brain. I gather words, try stringing them together, discard a few, and scramble for worthier ones. Not one of them will suffice. In fact, most of what I come up with is grossly inadequate. I need to convey brilliance, magnificence, stunning magic, novelty, a longing fulfilled, and blissful satisfaction. Even now, immersed in remembering something that happened a decade ago, my body tingles. Yes, of all the joyous times in my life, this moment changed me the most. It lifted my soul from lacking to content and complete.

What was about to spill from my lips was not fresh news to Robbie. She knows my story. She read my memoir, *Twice a Daughter*, which is the tale of the search for my birth relatives.

Like other readers, Robbie knows the basic facts of my adoption experience. But because she is not an adoptee or a birth mother, she cannot fully appreciate how my adoption search and reunion stack up against the other chapters in my life.

I say, "When each of my four children was born, I was ecstatic to see their little faces for the first time. I don't mean to minimize that time, but . . ."

"Go on. Share." Robbie demands and leans in.

I draw in my breath, and when I exhale, the words come. "The day I spoke to my birth mom on the phone for the first time . . . Hearing her voice after wondering for fifty years what it would sound like . . . After all the searching, and then the phone rang, and I was talking to *her*. As she talked, in my head I kept repeating: 'I'm talking to *her*. I'm actually talking to my mother.' I had fantasized about her for my entire life. And not only was she on the phone speaking with me, but she also sounded nice. And friendly. And loving. The more she talked, I had to close my eyes and open them right away to prove what was happening wasn't just a dream. Speaking to my birth mom was one of the happiest moments of my life."

I finish my little speech and collapse into the back of my rattan chair. Robbie reaches over, and her warm fingers close around my hand.

I smile back at her shyly and whisper, "And now it's your turn. What was your happiest moment?"

I listen as Robbie recounts her lovely story. I think about how good it feels to be sitting with a friend, sharing a fabulous lunch and a beautiful autumn day. I think about my friend's question and how wonderful it is to concentrate on only the happiest times.

Robbie's question is an elixir; it has transformed another Monday into a magical afternoon. I read somewhere that fear and gratitude occupy the same space in the brain, and if we want to banish our anxieties, we should think about something for which we are grateful. Today, I'm grateful for the bountiful supply of happy memories on which my life has been built.

EMPATHY: THE RIPPLE EFFECT

One of the questions I often field about my adoption search and reunion experience is how I coped with the initial devastating denial by my birth mother and the subsequent dismissal by my birth father. I always respond by talking about Catholic Charities, the agency that facilitated my closed adoption in 1959, and the institutional compassion this organization has consistently demonstrated throughout the course of my life. Empathy has a ripple effect. It allows us to feel supported, offers hope, and paves the way to forgiveness and healing.

Decades ago, Catholic Charities instituted a firm policy of placing children from a multiple-birth pregnancy into the same adoptive family. By strictly adhering to this guideline, the agency honored the attachment, established before we were born, between my sister and me. It also validated our belonging to one another and reinforced a unique relationship, which has proven integral to our formation of identity.

The bond I share with my twin blossomed during our formative years, and as we enter middle age, our connection is strong and true. Our relationship has always been unique, tight, and complicated. We finish each other's thoughts, communicate most effectively nonverbally, and often appear in social settings with similar outfits or accessories. We do not just "get" each other—it is as if we are stitched into the same skin.

In 2008, when I learned I needed a breast biopsy, my sister was my first phone call. We decided it was time to research our adoption and gather family medical history. She supported my need for information, and together we charted a course that stretched out for five years. At each juncture, we discussed options and decided upon next steps. She boosted me when I hesitated, doubted, or dipped into the gloom of disappointment. When we hit a milestone, we cheered the glorious achievement together. Without my twin sister, I am not me. Without her, my life journey would be a story less than half-told. And without her holding my hand as we crossed the finish line of our adoption search, the taste of victory would have been bitter and not honey sweet.

The incredible compassion demonstrated by Catholic Charities didn't stop with their insisting on adopting my sister and me into the same family. Through its Post-Adoption Services department, the organization continues to minister to me with respect to adoption-related issues such as identity, belonging, rejection, betrayal, and loss.

During our five-year adoption search and reunion process, I met quarterly with a support group made up of the adoption constellation: fellow adoptees, birth parents, adoptive parents, siblings, and significant others. Meeting regularly with this group introduced me to the diverse perspectives of others within the adoption world. I came to have empathy for the unique experience of birth parents, and for the challenges adoptive parents have in parenting. Much like my relationship with my twin sister, peer support has given me strength during my post-adoption adult life.

This condensed excerpt from my memoir, *Twice a Daughter: A Search for Identity, Family, and Belonging,* describes my first post-adoption support group meeting:

> The format of the meeting was simple. After signing in, we went around the U-shaped conference table and stated our name, disclosed whether we were an adoptee, birth parent, or adoptive parent, and then we shared where we were in the search and reunion process. If we brought someone with us, we introduced them.
>
> For the icebreaker piece, Lisa asked that we offer a response to this question: "If you could say one thing to the family member you seek, what would that be?"
>
> Ethnically and racially diverse, the group members ran the spectrum in age from thirtysomethings to seventy-year-olds. Except for two birth mothers, the rest were adult adoptees, and all but three were women. The common thread: Catholic Charities had facilitated everyone's adoption.
>
> More than half of us were waiting to hear back from a birth parent or birth daughter/son. From my experience of waiting weeks for my birth mom to answer my outreach, I knew how excruciating passing the time can be. A woman I guessed her to be in her late thirties had been anticipating a response from her birth mother for over a year. When she broke down in sobs during her introduction, the Kleenex box at the center of the table shot over to her like a hockey puck.

One of the birth mothers and a female adoptee shared their reunion stories. Both glowed like someone who'd recently fallen in love. They passed around photos of themselves beaming, wrapped in tight embraces with their newfound relatives. To the group's credit, each of us goggled at how much the searchers resembled their child or parent, and each attendee professed such joy and support for the searcher that I wondered why I'd postponed joining such a compassionate crowd.

When it was my turn to talk, I clasped my sweaty hands tightly in my lap. "I'm Julie. This is my first meeting. I'm an adoptee." I tried to make eye contact with the people across the table. "I also happen to be a twin. Thanks to Catholic Charities' policy of keeping twins together, my sister and I were adopted into the same family." I smiled at Lisa, our moderator, and then I looked down at the tabletop. "Due to health concerns, I began the search for my birth mother last year. Last month, I learned that she doesn't want to connect with us. I'm hoping she'll change her mind someday." When I glanced up, I caught the Kleenex box just in time.

The moderator jumped in. "And Julie, how would you answer the icebreaker question?"

The tissue balled up in my palm. I'd thought hard about this when the others spoke. The angry-rejected-adoptee me, the one I'd been working hard at controlling these days, wanted to ask my birth mom: how could she look herself in the mirror every day, she who gave up not one but two daughters and rejected both of us—twice? The person-that-was-me-before-this-adoption-search, the one I was desperately trying to reclaim 24/7, chose a different response to offer the group. "I would ask her if she has thought of my sister and me throughout her life, and if she ever wondered what had happened to us."

Due to COVID, my Catholic Charities post-adoption support group meets virtually rather than in person. Through this safe space, I have made lifelong friends, people with whom I shared an instant connection due to our shared experience. This format put me in conversation with birth mothers who provided valuable insights into the behavior and emotions of my own birth mother. Seeing adoption through her eyes gave me compassion for her role as an unwed mother in the 1950s. Because of my continued involvement in this group, I am a fierce advocate for peer support.

Recently I was a guest speaker on a panel of writers. During the Q&A portion, the question came up of where we find courage and resiliency. I mentioned my relationship with my sister and my reliance on the Catholic Charities support group. A woman whom I will call Sara raised her hand in the chat. She was joining us from Australia, which meant she had risen at dawn to connect to the meeting.

Sara shared that she is a birth mom and that she had read my memoir. Twice. Upon finishing it the first time, Sara wept. My story had awakened complicated, suppressed thoughts and emotions. Reading the book had provided steps for Sara to begin to heal from the trauma of her adoption loss.

To our cozy virtual group, Sara said, "When I got to the chapter in *Twice a Daughter* about the support group meeting, I realized I needed peer support. Right away. I hadn't known such therapy groups existed for women like me." Through her tears, Sara thanked me for writing my story.

Many of us struggle from the effects of our lived experiences. As we work to cope, accept, and heal from all that life throws our way, there are many benefits to be drawn from the support of like-minded peers, counselors, and therapists. Seeing through others' eyes fosters self-improvement. It enables relationships to gain momentum. Receiving compassion and offering empathy are not just gifts we offer to ourselves and others. The ripple effect is felt within the family unit, the community, and beyond. And it serves to strengthen our sense of belonging.

ACKNOWLEDGMENTS

I want to recognize Laurie Scheer, who helped me select, compile and edit the essays included in this collection. Without Laurie's stewardship and encouragement, *Belonging Matters* might still be lingering in my "pending projects" pile.

Kudos to Patricia, Libby, and my team at Muse Literary in Chicago for their able assistance in shepherding this manuscript from draft into publication. Full circle gratitude to Sara Connell for so many things: mentoring me early in my writing career; connecting me to website guru (and now trusted friend) Marsha Craig; supporting and promoting *Twice a Daughter;* and co-founding Muse Literary with Patricia Fors where *Belonging Matters* found a home.

I am deeply indebted to Andrew Tallackson at *The Beacher Newspapers* for taking me on as a columnist so many years ago, offering me a paid byline, and allowing the reprint of columns significant to this collection.

Many thanks to my fellow writers who offered essential comments on my writing: Evelyn LaTorre, Rikki Westerschulte, Kim Fairley, and Lynda Smith Hoggan. Finally, I offer deep appreciation to the family, kin, friends, neighbors, and readers who follow my work. Your avid support and continual feedback fuel me with purpose each and every day.

SOURCES

The following essays were originally published in slightly different form in the following print and online publications:

"Why Now, Why Wait, and Why Not" originally appeared on Adoption.com.

"The Only Thing My Father Gave Me," "The Importance of 'Personal Story'": Brevity Nonfiction Blog

"What to Say to Ridiculous People in Unbearable Situations": *Art in the Time of Unbearable Crisis,* ed. Stephanie Raffelock

"Empathy: The Ripple Effect": *Real Women Write: Seeing Through Her Eyes,* ed. Susan Schoch

Reproduced with permission from *The Beacher Newspapers:*

"A Mother Is Never Far," "The Nursing Fawn," "Who Is Your 'I'll Be Right Over' Friend?," "Finding Inspiration in an Unlikely Place," "You Never Know," "Mistakes and Forgiveness," "Favorite Son, Favorite Daughter," "Capturing Candid Moments," "My Mother's Words," "Fellowship and Favorite Family Phrases," "Planting Tulips," "Two Lessons Learned," "Savoring Holiday Celebrations," "Does Anyone Have a Cell Phone Charger?," "The Center of the Cinnamon Roll," "The Happiest Moment": *The Beacher Newspapers,* ed. Andrew Tallackson

ABOUT THE AUTHOR

J ulie Ryan McGue is an American writer. She is a domestic adoptee and an identical twin. Her award-winning memoir, *Twice a Daughter: A Search for Identity, Family, and Belonging,* was released in May 2021. It is about her five-year search to locate birth relatives, family medical history and personal background. In Julie's weekly blog and monthly column (*The Beacher Newspapers*), she writes about finding out who you are and where you belong and making sense of it. Her work has appeared in the *Story Circle Network Journal, Brevity Nonfiction Blog, Imprint News, Adoption.com, Lifetime Adoption Adoptive Families Blog, Adoption & Beyond,* and *Severance Magazine.* Her personal essays have appeared in several anthologies: *Real Women Write: Seeing Through Her Eyes* (Story Circle Network), and *Art in the Time of Unbearable Crisis* (She Writes Press, 2022).

Julie holds a BA in psychology from Indiana University and an MM in marketing and finance from the Kellogg Graduate School of Business, Northwestern University. She splits her time between northwest Indiana and Sarasota, Florida. She is a past board member for the Midwest Adoption Center, and she currently serves on the board of directors for the Center for American Family Building. Julie's second memoir (She Writes Press) launches in fall 2024.

FOLLOW JULIE HERE:

Author website: www.juliemcgueauthor.com
www.facebook.com/juliemcguewrites
www.twitter.com/juliermcgue
www.instagram.com/julieryanmcgue
www.goodreads.com/julieryanmcgue
www.linkedin.com/in/julie-mcgue-a246b841